How To Sue
Your Mother-In-Law
. . . And Prosecute
Your Kids

How To Sue Your Mother-In-Law ... And Prosecute Your Kids

Ready-To-Use Legal Letters To Terrorize Your Family

Andrew Harley

Michael O'Mara Books Limited

First published in Great Britain in 2007 by
Michael O'Mara Books Limited
9 Lion Yard, Tremadoc Road
London SW4 7NQ

A CIP catalogue record for this book is available from the British Library

ISBN: 978-1-84317-231-4

10 9 8 7 6 5 4 3 2 1

www.mombooks.com

Designed and typeset by Marc Burville-Riley

Printed and bound in Finland by WS Bookwell, Juva

Contents

Introduction

Does your wife spend longer on the phone than a call-centre operator? Does your husband require surgical removal from the remote control? Are your kids' demands for extortionate sums of pocket money severely damaging your bank balance? Or is your mother-in-law more of a monster-in-law? Now's the time to take action. You wouldn't think twice about asserting your rights and protecting your interests when it comes to sub-standard goods. But too many of us fail to take appropriate action in our own homes. And that is where *How To Sue Your Mother-In-Law* steps in to save the day. Packed full of cut-out-and-keep letters, forms and contracts, here you will find ready-made solutions to everyday domestic disasters.

There is something for every disgruntled member of the family within the pages of this book. Covering all aspects of dating and cohabiting, it contains forms to resolve (or ignite) domestic disputes aplenty. Women who find themselves lumbered with men whose personal hygiene routines resemble that of an orang-utan might want to issue them with Personal Hygiene Pledge Cards (see page 17). Husbands who find their wives are a little too plastic-happy might want to clamp down on this sort of reckless expenditure with a Food Shop Overspend Letter (page 37). Put-upon parents trying to discipline wayward adolescents will find a friend in the Acceptable Behaviour Contract (page 89): more personal than an ASBO, this contract will show your offspring who's boss . . . that is, of course, until they issue you with a Suing Your Parents Compensation Claim (page 103). The forms also deal with the most terrifying conflict of all: the perpetual struggle between the forces of Good and Evil – the Son- or Daughter-In-Law versus the Mother-In-Law.

The key over the page will help guide you when you are selecting forms. There are forms for boyfriends, girlfriends, husbands, wives, children and mother-in-laws to cut out and present to various members of the family whatever the occasion. So what are you waiting for? Domestic bliss is just a legal document away.

Key

SENDER

Male	Female	Parent	Child	Mother-in-law

RECIPIENT

Male	Female	Parent	Child	Mother-in-law

SUBJECT

Sex	Work	Money	Health	Romance	Lifestyle

CATEGORY

Imposing Rules	Asserting Rights	Sending to Doghouse	Making Complaints	Collecting Intelligence	Launching Nuclear Strike

Getting Together

GIRLFRIEND APPLICATION FORM

Sender:	Recipient:	Subject:	Category:
Male	Female	Romance	Collecting Intelligence

Guidance Notes:

Ideal for:
Finding a partner

When running a business, no one in their right mind would hire someone without finding out who else is available and selecting the best candidate. There is no reason why this approach shouldn't systematically be applied to relationships. It will sift out the non-starters, and you'll be able to evaluate their potential in the comfort of your own home.

Girlfriend Application Form

For a position with:

Full-Time ☐ Part-Time ☐ Job-Share ☐ REF NO

PERSONAL INFORMATION OF PROSPECTIVE GIRLFRIEND

Name:

Address:

Age: Status: Children: Income: Home Owner? (Y/N)

PHYSICAL CHARACTERISTICS
PLEASE INCLUDE RECENT PHOTOGRAPH/VIDEO

Vital Statistics: Height and Weight:

Ethnic Group: Piercings/Tattoos (Y/N)   Deformities (Y/N)

PERSONALITY PROFILE

Which of the following do you consider to be most romantic?

a) Chocolates & flowers   b) A walk in the country

c) Doing the dishes   d) An amorous threesome

Do you have a willing friend/accomplice? (Y/N)

(PHOTOGRAPH AND CONTACT DETAILS REQUIRED)

Have you remembered to enclose a medical certificate stating clean bill of
sexual health? (Y/N)

Please provide full details of any criminal convictions, violent incidents
against partners, etc., below. *Continue on a separate sheet if necessary.*

**Declaration: the information on this form is true to the best of my knowledge.
I confirm that I am of relatively sound mind.**

Signed and Dated:

Thank you for taking the time to complete this application. Please note that short-listed candidates will be invited to give a practical demonstration of their abilities. We regret that unsuccessful applications cannot be acknowledged due to a lack of administrative support.

BREEDING CERTIFICATE

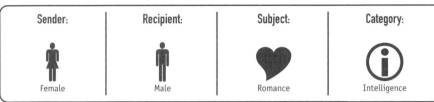

Sender:	Recipient:	Subject:	Category:
Female	Male	Romance	Intelligence

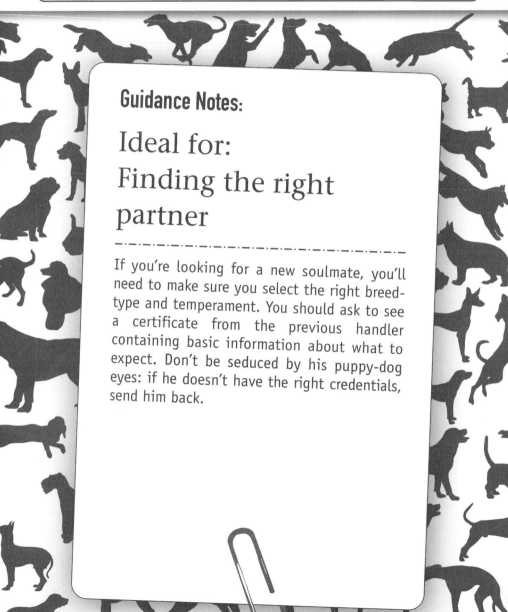

Guidance Notes:

Ideal for: Finding the right partner

If you're looking for a new soulmate, you'll need to make sure you select the right breed-type and temperament. You should ask to see a certificate from the previous handler containing basic information about what to expect. Don't be seduced by his puppy-dog eyes: if he doesn't have the right credentials, send him back.

Breeding Certificate

Breeder Name: *(insert surname)*

Personal Name: *(insert first name)*

Date of Birth:

• That the above has been certified as being of the following breed-type:
- ☐ Working   *Sought-after but hard to find*
- ☐ Pastoral   *A good 'homemaker', but a bit dull*
- ☐ Toy   *Great accessory but otherwise pointless*

• That he is placid/dependable/excitable in temperament and that he can/cannot be trusted to 'stay'/stay faithful/have an accident on the sofa *(delete as applicable)*.

• That in obedience trials, he has demonstrated an ability to understand and obey a series of verbal/non-verbal commands including the following:
- ☐ To walk to heel
- ☐ To respond to hand-signals
- ☐ To wait and come on command

• That he is mainly/moderately/not at all house-trained, and that he has learned not to chase birds/mount complete strangers/relieve himself in public places *(delete as applicable)*.

• Generally, he is manageable/frisky/uncontrollable and should/should never be let off the leash *(delete as applicable)*.

That in conclusion the above is considered suitable for:
    ☐ Breeding   ☐ Showing   ☐ Working   ☐ None of the above

Signed and Dated:

Please note: This certificate is only valid when bearing an official stamp.

Sender:	Recipient:	Subject:	Category:
Male	Female	Romance	Asserting Rights

Guidance Notes:

Ideal for: Returning unwanted goods

Dating agencies are an effective way of gaining access to suitable candidates for a relationship. Professional and discreet, they will do their best to find you the perfect partner in exchange for a tidy sum. Human sensibilities require that people should not be treated like electrical items or white goods, but the commercial basis on which agencies operate nevertheless gives you basic statutory rights. Remember that you should be able to return an item for whatever reason as long as it is in its original condition.

Return of Unwanted Item to Dating Agency

To: .... *(name of dating agency)*

On .... (dd/mm/yy), I took an interest in the following item:

....

(Please include the 'name' as well as a brief description of the item, e.g. 'white female medium height slim brunette brown eyes', & noting distinguishing marks, if any.)

During the initial period of inspection lasting ....

(state period of 'free trial'*), a problem has occurred that I wish to draw to your attention, namely, that the item is:

☐ Faulty ☐ Non-conforming

☐ Used (contrary to item description) ☐ Not the item I ordered

☐ Unsafe ☐ Other

Please provide additional details – including when and how the problem was discovered: ....

....

I now wish to *(please select one of the following)*:

☐ Have the problem put right

☐ Return the item and owe you nothing

☐ Return the item and exchange it for the following *(state 'name' and description of alternative)*:

....

I confirm that the item has been subject to normal use only and that the 'free-trial' period still applies. I have read and understood all relevant terms and conditions.

Signed and Dated:

....

Note: The term 'faulty' applies where an item is unable to function properly; the term 'non-conforming' applies where an item is *unwilling* to function properly.
*It is usual that once the parties begin to cohabit the 'free-trial' period shall automatically be deemed to have expired whereupon full payment is due and the standard no-return policy applies.

PERSONAL HYGIENE PLEDGE CARD

Sender:	Recipient:	Subject:	Category:
Female	Male	Health	Sending to Doghouse

Guidance Notes:

Ideal for: Avoiding cross-contamination

If you identify problems early on, you may wish to remind your partner of personal hygiene health-and-safety issues. Once you've helped him read through the accompanying form, get him to sign in the places indicated. Then tell him to make his own Pledge Card which should be proudly carried with him at all times. You may even be able to help him regain some self-respect.

Personal Hygiene Pledge Card

Name: Date of Birth: /   /

I confirm that I do NOT have any of the following foreign agencies residing anywhere on my person:

• Fleas/Ticks/Spider mites and any other known or unknown parasites
• Fungal infections affecting any or all surface areas and/or body crevices

I confirm that I do NOT have problems in regard to any of the following:

• Fermenting armpits   • Unwashed underpants
• Synthetic socks   • Industrial earwax

I confirm that I do NOT harbour active or dormant bacteria associated with gangrene, leprosy, syphilis or any other known bacterial disease.

Furthermore, I agree to carry the PLEDGE CARD below to remind me of my onerous duties and obligations:

Signed and Dated:

Instructions: (1) Cut out (2) Fold along centre (3) Stick together (4) Laminate

PERSONAL HYGIENE PLEDGE CARD

• I WILL WASH DAILY
• I WILL CHANGE MY UNDERPANTS
• I WILL USE DEODORANT

Name

Signature

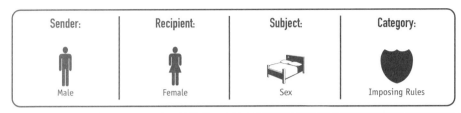

Sender:	Recipient:	Subject:	Category:
Male	Female	Sex	Imposing Rules

Guidance Notes:

Ideal for: Avoiding sexual misunderstandings

In today's climate, it's increasingly necessary for sexual boundaries to be clearly defined before it's too late. The solution in the United States is one that the rest of the world should follow, and consists of a straightforward agreement between the parties to minimize the possibility of misunderstandings or exploitation. This agreement covers all the essentials, including the opportunity for exclusions.

Sex Agreement

Between: _____ *(insert name)*

and: _____ *(insert name)*

SECTION A

That the PARTIES above do AGREE to indulge in SEXUAL RELATIONS for a period of _____*(state duration)* beginning at _____G.M.T. *(state time)* on _____ (dd/mm/yy).

Explicit CONSENT is given by the PARTIES in respect of the following activities:

- ☐ Manual Stimulation
- ☐ Oral Stimulation
- ☐ Visual Stimulation
- ☐ Video Recording
- ☐ Fetishism
- ☐ Anything Goes

Conversely, the following activity is expressly PROHIBITED:

_____

(State area of activity e.g. sadomasochism)

AND that the above TERMS will/will not apply in the event that either PARTY is tipsy/inebriated/unconscious *(delete as applicable)*.

SECTION B

Immediately prior to the expiry of the above AGREEMENT, the question may be put:

'Is it now your wish to renew the AGREEMENT on the same terms?'

A simple but emphatic 'YES' is sufficient as CONFIRMATION of the same.[1]

BOTH PARTIES SHOULD SIGN AND DATE THIS AGREEMENT BELOW:

_____

[1] It being generally impractical to obtain written consent at this junction.

DECLARATION OF INTENTION TO COMMIT

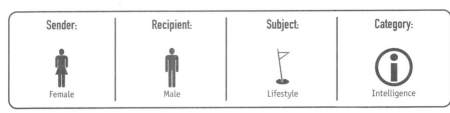

Sender:	Recipient:	Subject:	Category:
Female	Male	Lifestyle	Intelligence

Guidance Notes:

Ideal for: Identifying timewasters

It can be depressing to discover that you've been wasting your time unnecessarily when the love of your life walks out on you shortly after you've passed your prime. This Declaration of Intention to Commit will help sort the wheat from the chaff, requiring your partner to put things in black and white. It may be presented at any time, but ideally between a period of 3 months and 30 years after the relationship began.

Declaration of Intention to Commit

I, ... *(insert name)*, recognize that the object/victim of my affections has a right to know what my true intentions are at this stage in our relationship.

Given that we have now spent _____ weeks/months/years *(delete as applicable)* together, I understand that the other party in the relationship is entitled to have some input into planning the only life she will ever have in order to avoid wasting her time unnecessarily.

I am able to appreciate that she needs to make decisions about her career and family which cannot be left to pure chance. I now realize that it's not just about me: it's about us.

To this end, I hereby make an historic and courageous break with male psychology by actually making my intentions clear:

● I do/do not intend to acknowledge your existence in public before the age of 30/50/70 *(delete as applicable)*.

● I have/have not decided to issue you with a key to the flat in the next _____ months/years *(delete as applicable)*.

● It is/is not my wish for us to buy a house together *(delete as applicable)*. I will be making a mortgage application on _____ (dd/mm/yy).

● I will/will not be making a proposal of marriage to you in the next _____ weeks/months/years/decades *(insert number and delete as applicable)*.

● It is my ambition to have children with you in the next ____ months/years *(insert number and delete as applicable)*.

● I see you as my 'rock' – an enduring source of stability in an unpredictable universe/a stepping stone to something better *(delete as applicable)*.

I hereby make this solemn and truthful declaration.

Signed and Dated:

....

Witness's signature (1):

....

Witness's signature (2):

....

COHABITATION AGREEMENT

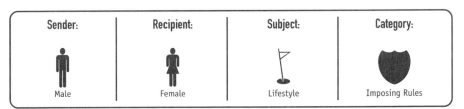

Sender:	Recipient:	Subject:	Category:
Male	Female	Lifestyle	Imposing Rules

Guidance Notes:

Ideal for: Laying down the ground rules

It is now widely recognized that if you cohabit, you need to make sure your interests are protected. One way to do this is through a Cohabitation Agreement that spells out your rights in black and white. Instead of paying a lawyer to complicate matters, you could use the standard document that follows – or amend the same as necessary. Explain to your partner that she will enjoy no rights at all unless she signs where indicated.

Cohabitation Agreement

Terms and Conditions for Living Together

THE PROPERTY
1.1 The PROPERTY shall be made available to the GIRLFRIEND/WIFE/HOME HELP/PA/UNDER-MANAGER (select preferred term) for SHELTER and as a place of WORK.

1.2 That SHE shall enjoy no RIGHTS over the PROPERTY whatsoever.

DUTIES
2.1 All FOOD shall consist of organic ingredients freshly prepared to the highest standard. The Dish of the Day should be produced by way of a RECIPE and should not consist of random combinations of ingredients thrown together. A duty of care is owed to members of the household not to prepare food likely to cause injury or distress.

2.2 Unwashed DISHES should never be in evidence with the SOLE exception of actual mealtimes.

2.3 The following areas should be cleaned DAILY: living room/dining room/hall/kitchen/bathroom/master bedroom/second bedroom/garage/loft (*delete as applicable*). DUST should be INVISIBLE to the naked eye.

2.4 Clothes, linen, etc., USED OR UNUSED should be washed, dried and ironed at least every day.

PRIVILEGES
3.1 STAFF shall be permitted to use the family car on condition that (a) the journey is for the benefit of the household and (b) SHE LEARNS HOW TO CHANGE GEAR.

SPECIAL MEASURES
4.1 Should any of the DUTIES in Section 2 (above) not be fully complied with, SPECIAL MEASURES may be introduced whereby teenage au pairs will be hired, whose tasks will be undefined and whose stay may be temporary or PERMANENT according to their performance.

CHILDREN
5.1 That SHE shall follow directions in all matters pertaining to the manufacture and maintenance of CHILDREN.

SEPARATION
6.1 That in the event of separation, the REMAINING occupant of the PROPERTY shall make all significant decisions in regard to the distribution of ASSETS, CHILDREN, etc.

6.2 That HE shall NEVERTHELESS make reasonable efforts to ensure that surplus GOODS are forwarded to HER new place of residence or to a HOSTEL/piece of land as applicable.

COMPLAINTS
7.1 That all COMPLAINTS shall be dealt with through the proper PROCEDURES and by the completion of an Official Complaints Form.

WE both AGREE to all of the above terms which shall be valid in perpetuity.

.... (dd/mm/yy)
Signature of Head of Household

.... (dd/mm/yy)
Signature of Female Cohabitee (Temporary Position)

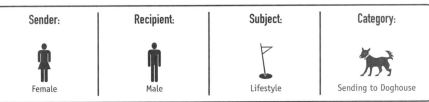

Sender:	Recipient:	Subject:	Category:
Female	Male	Lifestyle	Sending to Doghouse

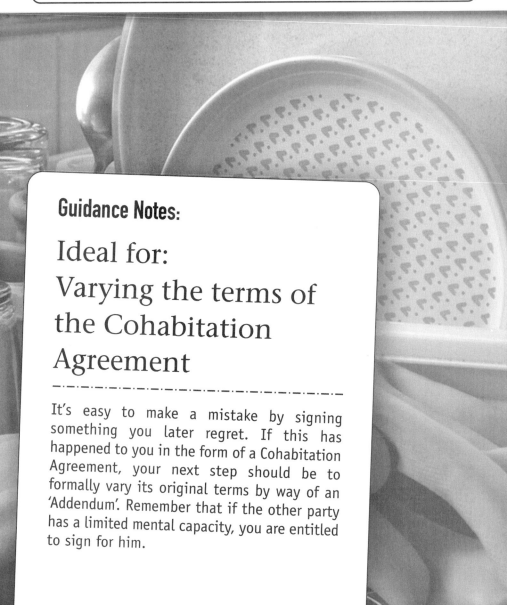

Guidance Notes:

Ideal for: Varying the terms of the Cohabitation Agreement

It's easy to make a mistake by signing something you later regret. If this has happened to you in the form of a Cohabitation Agreement, your next step should be to formally vary its original terms by way of an 'Addendum'. Remember that if the other party has a limited mental capacity, you are entitled to sign for him.

Addendum to Cohabitation Agreement

CHAUVINIST DRIVEL

That Sections 1–7 of 'the Agreement' should be STRUCK OUT. Generously summed-up by the technical term 'DRIVEL', they reflect nothing more than the state of the OTHER PARTY'S Neolithic mental functioning.

MISSING LINK

That attention is politely drawn to the recent revolution in the RIGHTS and STATUS of women over the past century or so. It may come as a shock to CERTAIN PARTIES to learn that the women who chained themselves to department store railings, circa 1910, were not campaigning for the right to go shopping. It appears that not only has the MISSING LINK between apes and humans been finally discovered, but that he is very much alive and kicking.

RE-EDUCATIVE PROGRAMMING

A well-documented feature of this archaic species is their extremely limited cranial capacity which accounts for their poor social skills and cultural illiteracy. Nevertheless, following an intensive course of re-educative programming, it may be possible to reform these evolutionary anomalies by demonstrating: (a) how to get things done; (b) a grasp of 'COMMON SENSE'; and (c) the advanced skill of 'MULTITASKING'.

'ASSUMED' AGREEMENT

In view of these developments, no formal agreement is in fact necessary. This is because there is an ASSUMED AGREEMENT: that the party conducting the training programme, as course tutor, will inevitably play the dominant role on a practical level for the duration.

WE both AGREE to the above VARIATION:

.... (dd/mm/yy)
Signed by Course Tutor

.... (dd/mm/yy)
Signed by the above on behalf of Neanderthal Man

PRENUPTIAL AGREEMENT

Sender:	Recipient:	Subject:	Category:
Male	Female	Romance	Asserting Rights

Guidance Notes:

Ideal for: Covering all eventualities

All marriages have their ups and downs and when you're ready to move on, you need to make sure that your interests are protected. One way to do this is with the aid of a Prenuptial Agreement. The specially patented clause included on the accompanying form is designed to ensure that your wishes cannot be overturned in the Courts. It may not be an easy task to get the agreement signed, however, unless you are lucky or canny enough to have an illiterate fiancée.

Prenuptial Agreement

Between: Party [1] (HUSBAND TO BE)

And: Party [2] (WIFE TO BE)

WHILST BOTH PARTIES are looking forward to the day of BLESSED UNION, the following terms are HEREBY AGREED by mutual consent:

UPON the day that both PARTIES

(a) RUN OUT OF CONVERSATION, and
(b) RESENT EACH OTHER'S CLOSE PROXIMITY

The relationship and marriage shall be pronounced dead.

WHEREUPON, PARTY [2] should neither act surprised nor become hysterical upon PARTY [1] locating and bringing home a suitable replacement item.

AND that in this event, BOTH PARTIES will agree to an amiable separation without the involvement of solicitors or decrees, WHEREUPON it is further agreed that PARTY [1] should keep *all PROPERTY ASSETS AND CASH* and that PARTY [2] should keep her make-up bag and clarinet/ ....
(delete and insert alternative, as applicable).

THAT the above terms are AGREED and BINDING notwithstanding any attempt(s) by the COURTS of England and Wales to defeat the clear intentions of the PARTIES.

Signed and Dated: (PARTY [1])

Signed and Dated: (PARTY [2])

Sender:	Recipient:	Subject:	Category:
		£	
Female	Male	Money	Collecting Intelligence

Guidance Notes:

Ideal for: Avoiding financial meltdown

Even if you think you're in love with your partner, don't make the mistake of tying the knot without checking your prospective spouse's credit rating. If you fail to do your research you could find that the knot is nothing less than a noose around your financial neck. He may well be generous, charming and fit, but it will pay dividends to remember that psychopathic spending disorders often come in nice packages.

Bank Reference for Fiancé

Dear: .... *(Bank Manager)*

SUBJECT OF CONFIDENTIAL ENQUIRY:

Account Holder: .... *(insert name of fiancé)*

Account Number __ __ __ __ __ __ __ __

Sort Code __ __ - __ __ - __ __

You will understand that I need to obtain a banking reference for the above customer so that an informed decision can be reached in respect of his suitability for marriage.

Please answer the following questions as fully as possible:

1. How long has the above customer held an account with you?

2. What is the account holder's 'credit rating'?

3. Does the account holder hold any significant assets?

4. Has the account holder ever been subject to any of the following?

   (a) Conviction for Fraud (b) Bankruptcy Order (c) Action for Repossession
   (If your answer is yes please mark 'FOR SHREDDING' in top right-hand corner.)

5. How much do you calculate is spent on the following on an average monthly basis?

   (a) Gambling: £__ __:__ __ (b) Sex DVDs: £__ __:__ __ (c) Alcohol: £ __ __:__ __

6. To what extent would you describe the above customer as a 'liability'?

   ....

7. If you were a betting man, which word or phrase would best describe the above?

   (a) A Dead Cert. (b) A Long Shot (c) A Donkey

Thank you for your cooperation in this delicate matter.

Sincerely yours,

....

Sender:	Recipient:	Subject:	Category:
Male	Female	Romance	Asserting Rights

Guidance Notes:

Ideal for: Starting as you mean to go on

Once you've tied the knot, a summary of marriage terms should be presented to the new post holder. As with so many aspects of a successful relationship, the emphasis should be on openness and transparency. Detailed explanatory notes are included at the base of the accompanying form.

Marriage Terms and Conditions

PRESENTED TO: *(the wife/new post-holder)*

Congratulations on accepting a key position within the marriage. It is my view that the ceremony and reception on .... (dd/mm/yy) went well/disastrously/as to be expected *(delete as applicable)*.

I now wish to take this opportunity to present you with the following:

SUMMARY OF INITIAL TERMS AND CONDITIONS OF MATRIMONY

1. Starting Allowance/Grade ....
2. Working hours per week ....
3. Annual Leave Entitlement ....
4. Health insurance (Y/N) ....
5. Life Cover *(Value)* ....

Please sign and date below to indicate that you have read and understood the above.

....

END OF FORM

- ✂ - - -

(PLEASE DETACH ALONG DOTTED LINE ABOVE AND DESTROY THIS PART OF THE FORM)

Explanatory notes:

1. Low initial allowance always recommended. Any rises can be linked to inflation but note 'real terms' increase is unwise without proven efficiency savings.
2. Ninety hours per week core time is recommended. Flexi-sheets are easy to check and nurture a sense of responsibility and trust – the key to a good working relationship.
3. At your discretion, or mark as 'not applicable'.
4. A good way to protect your investment.
5. A good way to insure against any loss.

First
Strike

Sender:	Recipient:	Subject:	Category:
Male	Female	Work	Making Complaints

Guidance Notes:

Ideal for: Combating poor performance

Don't make the mistake of allowing standards to slide. Ideally, your partner should have signed a Cohabitation Agreement, which obviously makes it easier to identify and deal effectively with any breach. However, it is a fact that most people don't know what documents they've signed – and your partner is probably no different. In the unlikely event that you are challenged on the minutiae of the detail contained within your letter, you can always claim that 'the Agreement' is assumed and merely confirms basic Health and Safety legislation – any breach of which will be dealt with severely by the authorities.

Sub-standard Housework

Dear: *(name of wife or partner)*
....

On __/__/__ (dd/mm/yy) I carried out the usual weekly cleanliness and hygiene check and I was dismayed to find evidence of sub-standard housework in the living room/dining room/hall/kitchen/master bedroom/second bedroom/bathroom/garage/loft *(delete as applicable)*.

Research has shown that once standards begin to slide they can become impossible to recover. It also carries serious health and safety implications. As you are aware, I have a duty to ensure that all staff enjoy a safe working environment.

To this end, I feel I must draw your attention to the following:

- ☐ Arachnid discovered in bath
- ☐ Stained mug found in cupboard
- ☐ Old dust found in vacuum cleaner
- ☐ Grease mark obscuring view from landing window
- ☐ Cobwebs discovered in loft

I should point out that other people are also affected by your carefree attitude. Only the other day, I turned up at work to find that my shirt/ trousers/tie/shoes were unironed/unpressed/unpolished *(delete as applicable)*. This was personally devastating for me and I felt that I had really let my team down.

I attach photographic evidence of the above by way of the following exhibits: *(insert 'A', 'B', 'C', etc.)*
....

I trust that improvements will materialize before I am forced to arrange for a Performance Review, which you should pencil into your diary for twenty-eight days from today.

Sincerely yours,

....
Encl: exhibits

Sender:	Recipient:	Subject:	Category:
Male	Female	Money	Making Complaints

Guidance Notes:

Ideal for: Budgeting

Even marginal overspending on common shopping items can cost the earth if it becomes a frequent occurrence. It can cripple the household financially and lead to family conflict. A formal letter sent at an early stage can prevent bad habits forming. Problem areas, such as spending on shoes, can be identified – and the requirement for your partner to provide a small presentation demonstrating improved spending habits will compel her to change her behaviour and show that there has been an improvement. Once an understanding of the Retail Price Index has been grasped, your partner should be able to budget more effectively.

Food Shop Overspend

Dear: .... *(name of wife or partner)*

I have checked your shopping receipts for the last .... *(state number)* weeks/months/years *(delete as applicable)* and it appears that you have failed to keep expenditure within prudent levels.

For your information, food shopping has increased by .... % over the last .... months/years. Expenditure on other items, namely

....

.... *(state items such as shoes, clothes, etc.)*, has similarly increased significantly/exponentially at a rate of .... %.

You should be aware that the RPI *(Retail Price Index)* for the same period has been .... %. Please study the accompanying graphs, which track your expenditure on a basket of goods against a full RPI breakdown for the same period. I can only assume that such reckless behaviour is linked to specific problems such as disordered thinking, emotional trauma or hormonal imbalance.

You have twelve weeks to turn things around, following which you will need to demonstrate significant improvement by making a small presentation to the family. It would be devastating for me to have to refer you for specialist help, not to mention the embarrassment it will cause the family.

Sincerely yours,

....

Encl: graphs showing above data

Sender:	Recipient:	Subject:	Category:
Male	Female	Health	Making Complaints

Guidance Notes:

Ideal for: Combating poor performance

This letter is designed to be multi-purpose, in that a number of different scenarios are addressed. Just tick the boxes that apply in your particular case, and be sure to provide evidence, including photographs, as necessary. Don't expect to see immediate improvement, however: low morale could be the cause of the original problem – so you should be sensitive to the needs of kitchen staff. Give genuine encouragement, even where improvement has been minimal, and don't forget to compliment the new high standards should the opportunity arise.

Sub-standard Food

Dear: *(name of wife or partner)*
....

On .... (dd/mm/yy), the family sat down for the .... o'clock
serving of breakfast/lunch/tea/dinner *(delete as applicable)*.

I/ .... *(or state member of family)* was dismayed to find
that, upon tasting the dish described as .... *(state dish)*,
it was found to be sub-standard for the following reason:

☐ The dish carried an unusually poor flavour
☐ The dish was cold
☐ The dish was so hot as to present an obvious health and safety risk
☐ The dish contained a foreign body of unknown
   origin/recognized as:

....

....

The foreign body so described is attached herewith as 'Exhibit A'
(strike out if not applicable).

As you are aware, the Food Safety Act 1990 makes it a criminal offence
to supply food not of 'the nature, substance or quality demanded'. You
also owe a special duty of care to members of your family not to
administer poison.

Compensation has been set at a level of £ .... *(insert amount)*, which
should be paid by 12 noon on .... (dd/mm/yy).

Sincerely yours,

Sender:	Recipient:	Subject:	Category:
Male	Female	Health	Making Complaints

Guidance Notes:

Ideal for: Combating non-performance

Don't forget that your partner may have to juggle many different commitments – from domestic duties to childcare to part-time work. Having said that, food is an essential ingredient for life and a missed meal can lead to energy deficiencies that carry serious health and safety implications. It is also a breach of human rights. Improvisation, where attempted, carries its own risk. These combined factors mean you shouldn't shy away from early, formal, action to prevent the problem spiralling out of control. A dual-action carrot and stick remedy is required in the form of a straightforward demand for compensation plus an unexpected gesture or peace offering – such as initiating a project to redesign the menus.

Absence of Food

Dear: *(name of wife or partner)*

On .... (dd/mm/yy), I seated myself in readiness for the standard serving of breakfast/lunch/tea/dinner *(delete as applicable)*.

Despite my prompt arrival, I was informed that no booking existed in my name. Considerable embarrassment and inconvenience ensued as I was forced to improvise despite:

☐ Having a paper cut on my right/left/finger/thumb *(delete as applicable)*
☐ Being unable to find any ingredients
☐ Having had no formal training

Eventually, it was necessary to obtain nourishment elsewhere in order to sustain normal energy levels.

Your failure to prepare and serve food constitutes a breach of contract and I am entitled to compensation as a result. Considering the humiliation and subsequent additional costs involved in travelling to and attending the local restaurant/fast-food establishment *(delete as applicable)*, I consider £ .... to be a reasonable sum.

Failure to deliver payment to me within the next 7 days will leave me with no option but to pursue a claim in the County Court, a step which would carry with it additional costs.

Sincerely yours,

Sender:	Recipient:	Subject:	Category:
Male	Female	Health	Making Complaints

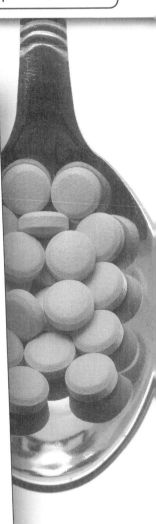

Guidance Notes:

Ideal for: Addressing health and safety concerns

No business could get away with serving up dangerous products day in, day out to unsuspecting customers – yet this is precisely what happens in many households up and down the country. Although, technically, your household cannot be closed down, a recent awareness of Health and Safety issues requires a basic standard of service even in the home. Strictly speaking, you could be held liable for injury even in the case of an elderly or unusually delicate victim.

Food Poisoning

Dear: _____ *(name of wife or partner)*

It was with some excitement that the extended family assembled from far and wide for my/your/the mother-in-law's anniversary/birthday *(delete as applicable)* with buffet lunch last _____ *(state day)*.

You will recall that after a short speech/slideshow/cabaret *(delete as applicable)*, expectations were running high as you brought out an ambitious selection of homemade food and invited the most senior members of the party to take first pick.

In retrospect, this was an obvious mistake, for within the space of a few seconds/minutes *(delete as applicable)*, the first victim was struck down with food poisoning.

Even though the autopsy revealed a digestive tract well past its sell-by date, the £300-per-hour consultant expressed genuine surprise at the chain reaction set in motion by the dish you described as:

_____ *(state dish)*.

Subsequent incidents were trivial in comparison, but the use of A&E services/hospitalisation *(delete as applicable)* still represents a drain on an already overstretched NHS – and I suggest that you pay a little more attention to food preparation next time round.

Apart from the above, I thought the occasion was a surprising success.

Sincerely yours,

_____

PARKING PERMIT

Sender:	Recipient:	Subject:	Category:
Male	Female	Lifestyle	Imposing Rules

Guidance Notes:

Ideal for:
Improving skills

Introducing a parking-permit system can give you more control over bad practice in the area of parking and driving. A white box can be painted onto the parking area outside the house or in the garage. You should not fail to patrol the area regularly, an inconvenience which can be compensated for by the revenue raised.

Parking Permit

REGISTRATION NUMBER:

....

PERMIT HOLDERS should note that the following terms STRICTLY apply:

1. Failure to display the permit will result in the vehicle being clamped/ towed away subject to a £................... release fee *(delete and/or insert amount as applicable)*.

2. When you attempt to park, it is recommended that you use the FIRST and REVERSE gears in order to reduce the likelihood of collision. Please note the convenient location of rear-view and wing mirrors, not to be confused with vanity mirrors.

3. You are required to position the ENTIRE vehicle within the marked bays only. Look out for the painted box at ground level outside the house/inside the garage *(delete as applicable)*.

4. The vehicle must at no time obstruct ACCESS to the house, whether via the front door or other entrance. As a general guide, keep the vehicle off soft verges/narrow paths/flower beds/bicycles/pedestrians *(delete as applicable)*.

5. In the event that the vehicle is parked successfully, take care to remove children or other animals BEFORE securing the vehicle.

6. As per this agreement, you will pay £................... *(insert amount)* for this PERMIT, which may/may not *(delete as applicable)* be subject to automatic deduction from your weekly allowance.

Please note that this PERMIT may be withdrawn at any time without reason and without notice.

....

Encl: ONE PARKING PERMIT

SELF-ASSESSMENT FORM

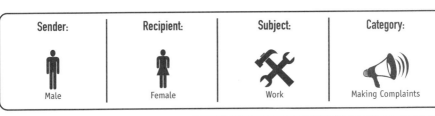

Sender:	Recipient:	Subject:	Category:
Male	Female	Work	Making Complaints

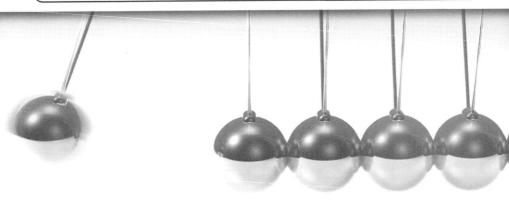

Guidance Notes:

Ideal for: Self-assessment and evaluation

The revolution in business culture over the past generation has provided a systematic approach to getting the most out of your staff. The following form uses the same strategy in relation to your partner, providing the opportunity for her to gain insight into problem areas within a sympathetic and supportive environment.

Self-Assessment Form
Helping Her to Drive Up Standards

Post: .... *(e.g. 'Housewife')*

Name of Post Holder: .... *(Wife/Partner)*

Name of Supervisor: .... *(head of household)*

Location: .... *(state address)*

Performance Appraisal: *This is your opportunity to be honest in assessing your own performance in-post.*

How do you feel you have performed in the following areas?
(Score yourself 1–5 in the boxes, following the key* for additional guidance)

Washing ☐   Cooking ☐   Dusting ☐   Vacuuming ☐

* Below-par = '1'   Sloppy = '2'   Inadequate = '3'   Slipshod = '4'   Diabolical = '5'

Team Culture: *This section is about improving the working relationship between management and personnel.*

How does an irrational resistance to change undermine any realistic chance of raising productivity via the 'Team Culture' model?

Competencies and Capabilities: *Not applicable*

Weaknesses Inventory:
Please rank the following factors in terms of how they contribute to poor performance

☐ Destructive attitude

☐ Volatile temperament

☐ Failure to recognise other people's strengths

(Now identify other relevant factors on additional sheets.)

Thank you for filling in this form. We hope it has been a positive and rewarding experience.

Sender:	Recipient:	Subject:	Category:
Male	Female	Lifestyle	Making Complaints

Guidance Notes:

Ideal for: Outmanoeuvring your adversary

Try not to respond in kind when your partner makes a complaint in an unusually vociferous manner about some aspect of your relationship. Remain calm and handle the matter in a dignified and professional way, explaining why a formal procedure needs to be followed. This is also an opportunity to point out that the process can only consider the merits of one case at a time.

Response to Complaint

Dear: _____ *(name of wife or partner)*

On _____ (dd/mm/yy) you made a complaint about some aspect of our relationship. As I recall, you stated that _____ and that I was a _____.

I am sorry if your stay here has been less than satisfactory. You are entitled to complain, but any points you raise should be made formally in writing. I regret that unofficial complaints cannot be processed due to the absence of documentation. This element may appear irksome, but it is essential for Quality Control purposes, the mechanism by which a First Class service can be delivered to future residents.

Considerable effort has been put into designing the attached Complaint Form, which invites you to set out in detail the merits of your case *(where applicable)*. You need to complete all sections and return the form to me, with documentation, in the envelope marked CONFIDENTIAL.

You will receive an acknowledgement card within seven days, although the full administrative process will take some months to complete. In the interim, it is essential that you do not raise any of the issues that are subject to investigation in order to avoid jeopardizing a fair trial.

Thank you for taking the trouble to complain.

Sincerely yours,

_____

Encl: Official Complaint Form with envelope

OFFICIAL COMPLAINT FORM

Sender:	Recipient:	Subject:	Category:
Male	Female	Lifestyle	Making Complaints

Guidance Notes:

Ideal for:
Buying time

Some people enjoy complaining and would jump at the chance of filling in an Official Complaint Form. This example gives your partner ample opportunity to make a complaint in a satisfying and gratuitous way. The complainant will feel empowered, thus giving the impression that her views are being taken on board. It can also offer useful pointers towards the underlying reasons for this pattern of behaviour: your partner may gain fresh insight into her character flaws and psychopathic tendencies, where applicable.

Official Complaint Form

Section 1
The following details are necessary for official purposes.

Miss/Mrs/Ms/Other:　　　First Name:　　　　　　　Surname:

....

Date of Birth:
....

Special requirements
We have tried to make this form as simple and easy to use as possible. However, if you find it difficult to understand plain English, please explain exactly how you expect us to help you.

Section 2*
* This section is *not* concerned with your mental health history.
1. Which member of the household are you complaining about this time?
2. What do you think he did wrong?
3. When exactly did this occur?
4. What time of the month was that?

Section 3
This section is about how the experience has affected you.
1. How did the experience affect you?
2. What do you think the person concerned should do to put things right?
3. Do you think it's reasonable to expect people to meet unrealistic expectations?
4. Did you give the person concerned a chance to put their side of the story?
5. Have you ever tried to look at a problem from someone else's perspective?
6. Are you familiar with the word 'compromise'?
7. How might you consider changing your behaviour in the future?

Section 4
This section is about complaining as a 'strategy for change'.
1. How often do you complain?
2. When you complain, do you think it makes any difference to anything?
3. Has it ever occurred to you that complaining is an ineffective strategy for change?
4. How could 'polite requests' or 'lobbying' be seen as constructive alternatives?

Section 5
This section is about evidence and documentation.
Which type of evidence have you supplied with this form?

☐ Sound recording evidence　　　☐ Photographic evidence

☐ Transcripts of conversations　　☐ Other: ....

Declaration
I declare that the information I have provided on this form is true – always bearing in mind the fact that one person's perspective is by definition narrow and biased.

Signed and Dated:

....

Sender:	Recipient:	Subject:	Category:
Male	Female	Lifestyle	Making Complaints

Guidance Notes:

Ideal for:
Achieving closure

It is important to be seen to be dealing with complaints properly, however groundless the tedious details of the case. This letter is sensitive to your partner's concerns, but also achieves closure – thus allowing you both to move forward. If you find that the whole complaints procedure is still taking up too much time, introduce extortionate administration charges.

Result of Investigation

Dear: _____ *(name of complainant)*

I am pleased to be able to inform you that after a period of ....weeks/months/years *(delete as applicable)*, your complaint, Reference No: __ __ __ *(insert number)*, has now been fully investigated in accordance with the Household's Complaints Procedures.

Having spent valuable time and resources looking into the matter with customary thoroughness, I regret that your complaint has been dismissed. The matter has now been fully investigated and the case is therefore closed.

I trust that you have, at least, gained some satisfaction from airing your grievance, and it may be that your comments will be taken on board in some way or another despite carrying little or no merit.

Please sign and date the attached copy of this letter to confirm that you have read and understood its contents, and return it to me, by hand, within the next seven days.

Sincerely yours,

_____

Encl: copy letter

Sender:	Recipient:	Subject:	Category:
Male	Female	Lifestyle	Making Complaints

Guidance Notes:

Ideal for:
Making a point

Sometimes it's impossible to find the words for genuine compliments and you find it difficult to articulate exactly what you want to convey. If one or more of the accompanying phrases fits the bill, tick the box or boxes. You don't even need to engage in conversation.

With Compliments

I'm not normally one to throw compliments about, but on:

- ☐ MONDAY
- ☐ TUESDAY
- ☐ WEDNESDAY
- ☐ THURSDAY
- ☐ FRIDAY
- ☐ SATURDAY
- ☐ SUNDAY

I couldn't help noticing:

- ☐ That your hair looked 'nice', which was just as well given that your trip to the salon cost the equivalent of 50 cataract operations in the developing world.

- ☐ The original and creative way in which food ingredients were thrown together at random to make the dish of the day.

- ☐ That your skin was noticeably younger-looking in low light, with visible lines, pockmarks and craters reduced by about 5 per cent.

- ☐ How much you enjoyed your work as you slammed plates, cutlery and condiments onto the kitchen table.

- ☐ How confidently you found the reverse gear, when driving at 50mph.

- ☐ How effortlessly you were able to put on your make-up at the same time as driving and engaging in mindless conversation.

- ☐ How conclusively you broke the world record for a single telephone conversation at 4 hours, 31 minutes and 6 seconds during peak time.

Sincerely yours,

....

Retaliation

Sender:	Recipient:	Subject:	Category:
Female	Male	Lifestyle	Making Complaints

Guidance Notes:

Ideal for:
Home truths

When you make the effort yourself but other people can't even be bothered to do the simplest things no matter how many times you remind them, you wonder why you bother at all. If you find yourself repeating the same things day in, day out, as you would to a small child, you might need to approach the problem from a different angle. Pay your husband or boyfriend a special compliment using the accompanying form.

With Compliments (2)

I'm not normally one to throw compliments about, but on:

- ☐ MONDAY
- ☐ TUESDAY
- ☐ WEDNESDAY
- ☐ THURSDAY
- ☐ FRIDAY
- ☐ SATURDAY
- ☐ SUNDAY

I couldn't help noticing:

☐ The hard work you put into changing TV channels.

☐ The uncharacteristic way in which you attempted to harness the latest technology (soap) in a hapless attempt to overcome body odour.

☐ The personal courage you showed in calling out a qualified mechanic in order to put back together the pieces of the family car after your attempt to fix it went wrong.

☐ The commitment you have shown to private study and research into X-rated Internet sites.

☐ The exacting standards you applied to washing and cleaning the car, whilst completely trashing the inside of the house.

☐ Your business acumen as you purchased yet another fitness accessory to add to your vast and unused collection, presumably in readiness to open a Health Club.

☐ How open you were about expressing human emotions and not being afraid to cry – especially when there was a goal.

Sincerely yours,

CUSTOMER NOTICE (HOME LAUNDERETTE)

Sender:	Recipient:	Subject:	Category:
Female	Male	Work	Imposing Rules

Guidance Notes:

Ideal for: Educating your clientele

Even these days, it's not unusual for chauvinistic males to mistake their partner for a live-in maid, especially in relation to washing duties. A discreet notice situated in an obvious place will serve to clear up any misunderstandings. Don't be fooled by confused mutterings about not knowing which settings to use, and be wise to attempts to sabotage the results by mixing colours and shrinking garments: these are all perfectly predictable responses to a newly hostile regime.

Customer Notice
(Home Launderette)

1. Identification of Machinery

Even inexperienced users should be able to identify the facility known as the WASHING MACHINE without assistance. It is the large white metal box with a round, hinged door on the front.

2. Suitable Items

It is recommended that only clothes, linen, etc., be placed inside the washing machine. Whilst attempts to clean crockery and cutlery are commendable, these items should properly be deposited inside the DISHWASHER, which is a different facility.

3. Manual Loading

Clothes, linen, etc, are NOT conveyed automatically to the washing machine. Despite the popular misconception, there is no 24-hour continuous collection service.

4. Technical Programming

Once you have successfully conveyed items from the floor, etc. to the washing machine, you are now ready to instigate technical programming. Don't worry your head trying to understand all aspects of the control panel: just load some powder and press the ON switch. If you wish to become an advanced user, enrol on an evening course.

5. Health and Safety

Soiled clothes, linen, etc, should not be left for an indefinite period before being washed. It is your responsibility to ensure that hazardous substances are properly treated so as to minimize the danger to other members of the household. This may necessitate the hiring of a subcontractor.

6. Charges

A basic service is delivered free at the point of use, but there will be a cost involved should any of the above terms not be fully complied with. This will involve the random re-arrangement of your physical anatomy.

7. Disclaimer

Whilst every care is taken to ensure that customers' articles are undamaged, some garments may completely disintegrate once dirt, food, bodily discharge, etc., has been broken down by the washing process. No responsibility will be accepted for resulting losses. Customers should also note that the question of whether serviced items should ever be worn in public is a matter of individual taste or lack thereof.

By Order of the Manager: *(insert signature here)*

Sender:	Recipient:	Subject:	Category:
 Female	Male	Work	Sending to the Doghouse

Guidance Notes:

Ideal for: Dealing with complaints

If your partner has been making unhelpful comments or complaints about food preparation, it may be time to launch a customer-satisfaction survey. This form sets out service provision and invites ideas on further improvement. Once the forms are completed, use them as a substitute for rice paper in homemade confectionery in order to drive your point home. Further complaints may constitute provocation, and legal justification to commit assault.

Home Restaurant Satisfaction Survey

Always Delighting Our Customers

Dear Customer

You may have noticed me around the home from time to time, preparing and serving food 24/7. My role is to produce generous portions of home-cooked sustenance for little or no reward. Service provision has been divided up into three core areas:

• Quality – It is my personal aim to ensure that all ingredients are rigorously checked for quality before being thrown together to make the dish of the day. All ingredients are positively identified, washed with soap and boiled for six hours before being passed as fit for almost-human consumption.

• Choice – No self-respecting customer wants to eat the same thing day-in day-out – and this is precisely why an entirely new dish is cobbled together once every Quarter.

• Service – With twenty years of food preparation behind me, I know the value of good service with a smile. It's the little things that matter, like eye contact and friendly remarks – even when the customer is too drunk or ignorant to notice or to make any effort himself.

I know how busy you are – with your hectic lifestyle and everything – but your ideas on improving the service even further really do matter. Perhaps you'd like proper waitresses, or dimmed lighting, or a separate bar area with air-conditioning. Please add your comments below. It will help if you arrange words into meaningful sentences.

Sender:	Recipient:	Subject:	Category:
Female	Male	Romance	Making Complaints

Guidance Notes:

Ideal for:
Insensitive partners

The scenario of the missed birthday or anniversary is sadly all too common, even among partners who have been together for many years and who should know better. This standard letter deals with the main points directly and succinctly, and carries more weight than another tirade of verbal abuse.

Missed Birthday/Anniversary

Dear: .... *(name of husband or partner)*

I was disappointed to note that you missed my birthday/our anniversary *(delete as applicable)*.

For your information, it was on .... (dd/mm/yy).

This was a special day for me/us *(delete as applicable)* and I don't understand why it should be so difficult for you to remember it. It's not as if it changes from year to year.

I hazard a guess that you missed it this time because:

☐ You suffered another attack of amnesia.

☐ You mixed me up with someone else.

☐ You overslept for the entire day.

If it's not beyond your capabilities, please explain to me in writing (a) how you intend to put things right, and (b) why it should be any different next year? I advise you not to leave it until 'later' as we both know the difficulties you have with advanced concepts such as past, present and future – otherwise known as 'time'.

Sincerely yours,

....

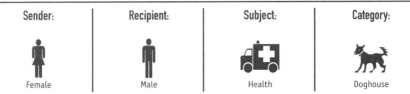

Sender:	Recipient:	Subject:	Category:
Female	Male	Health	Doghouse

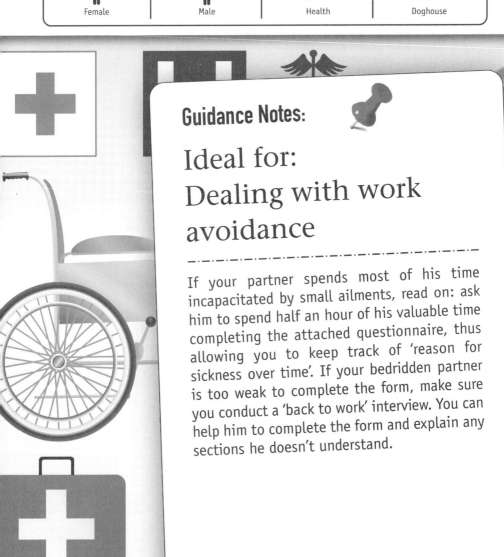

Guidance Notes:

Ideal for:
Dealing with work avoidance

If your partner spends most of his time incapacitated by small ailments, read on: ask him to spend half an hour of his valuable time completing the attached questionnaire, thus allowing you to keep track of 'reason for sickness over time'. If your bedridden partner is too weak to complete the form, make sure you conduct a 'back to work' interview. You can help him to complete the form and explain any sections he doesn't understand.

Self-Certification (Sickness)

Dear: .... *(name of wife or partner)*

Name of Post Holder: .... *(name of husband or partner)*

Location: .... *(state address)*

First Day of Sickness   _ _/_ _/_ _   (dd/mm/yy)

Last Day of Sickness   _ _/_ _/_ _   (dd/mm/yy)

Total Days of Sickness   _____   *(insert number)*

Please state why it was necessary for you to spend a whole day/week/month/year/decade *(delete as applicable)* lounging around at home expecting me to wait on you hand and foot.

So which disease was it this time?
Please tick appropriate box.

☐ Paper cut   ☐ Snuffly nose

☐ Stubbed toe   ☐ Alcohol poisoning

☐ RSI* to arm/thumb/wrist

☐ Other *(please state)* ....

*Typical causes of 'Repetitive Strain Injury' include beer-glass-lifting/fiddling with TV remote/no prizes.

How has the disease affected your ability to manage ordinary day-to-day tasks?
Please tick appropriate box.

☐ It's made no difference. I did very little in the first place.

Thank you for completing this confidential form, which will be shredded before being carefully filed.

Sender:	Recipient:	Subject:	Category:
Female	Male	Sex	Making Complaints

Guidance Notes:

Ideal for: Non-performance

It's not uncommon for men to suffer from performance difficulties once they have consumed an excessive quantity of alcohol. If this becomes habitual, a direct approach is required. You have the right to receive services from properly-equipped personnel – and this letter requires your partner to take appropriate action.

Intoxication on the Job

Dear: ....
(name of husband or partner)

As you may or may not remember, your performance in bed on .... *(state day)* was distinctly unsatisfactory. Certain vital equipment on your person was rendered non-operational due to excessive consumption of alcohol.

I had taken all reasonable steps to correct the problem, including ....
.... *(state steps taken)*, but without success.

I must point out that this is not an isolated incident. In fact, you have been unable to perform for this reason on .... *(state number)* separate occasions in the past week/month/quarter *(delete as applicable)*.

In future, it is essential that you are able to rise to the occasion if you wish to remain in-post.

Sincerely yours,

....

Please detach the tear off slip below and return to sender within 7 days.

--✂---------

DECLARATION

Please demonstrate to me your good intentions by reading over the statements that follow and placing your signature below by way of agreement.

1. I DO NOT INTEND TO SABOTAGE OUR RELATIONSHIP
2. I AM CAPABLE OF FINDING YOU ATTRACTIVE WITHOUT BEING BLIND DRUNK
3. I AGREE TO STOP DRINKING BEFORE BECOMING UNCONSCIOUS

(dd/mm/yy)

....

AMNESIAC MAN WORKSHEET

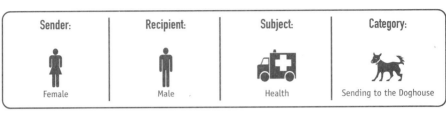

Sender:	Recipient:	Subject:	Category:
Female	Male	Health	Sending to the Doghouse

Guidance Notes:

Ideal for: Teaching memory skills

If, like a small child, your partner endlessly needs to be reminded about everything, you ought to go back to basics. Research shows that a memory deficit can be countered by an intensive learning programme. Like any form of teaching, it's important to praise the tiniest advances whilst pretending that the whole thing is fun. Change the colour of the worksheet occasionally in order to maintain interest, and eventually you may achieve a breakthrough – although this isn't by any means guaranteed.

Amnesiac Man Worksheet

Please follow the steps below:

1. Do you have any 'THINGS TO REMEMBER TO DO'?
2. Try to make a list of these in your weekly planner (below)
3. If you manage to complete the task, draw a happy face in COLUMN B
4. Remember to hand in your worksheet at the end of each week

	A Things to remember to do	B Done	C Date verified
MON			
TUE			
WED			
THU			
FRI			
SAT			
SUN			

EXAMPLES:

- Get up in the morning
- Wash
- Shave with your eyes open
- Apply for proper jobs

Remember – DON'T FILL IN COLUMN C.
That's for your supervisor when she marks your work.

Sender:	Recipient:	Subject:	Category:
Female	Male	Sex	Asserting Rights

Guidance Notes:

Ideal for:
Putting your foot down

When sexual interest is unwanted, inappropriate comments and gestures can be employed. If the person exhibiting this behaviour is your partner, you may need to work through some issues together. In the interim, however, you shouldn't have to put up with what amounts to sexual harassment. Citing a major authority such as the United Nations will help you make your point.

Sexual Harassment

Dear: _____ *(name of husband or partner)*

It has come to my attention that there has been an alarming rise in incidents of inappropriate behaviour.

It is my duty to remind you that the United Nations definition of sexual harassment is ' . . . any unwelcome sexual advance, request for sexual favour, or other verbal or physical conduct [creating] an intimidating, hostile or offensive environment.' I believe that this is an accurate description of our home.

I refer to your actions on _____ (dd/mm/yy), when you insulted me with the following behaviour *(please select)*:

- ☐ Touching
- ☐ Patting
- ☐ Pinching
- ☐ Leering
- ☐ Making predatory comments *(please state)*:

_____

_____

I believe I have made clear over a long period of time my complete disinterest in your advances, gestures, hints and comments. If you are in any doubt, you should assume that your actions are inappropriate and that your feelings are unreciprocated.

Sincerely yours,

Sender:	Recipient:	Subject:	Category:
Female	Male	Lifestyle	Sending to Doghouse

Guidance Notes:

Ideal for: Gardening tips

Having a well-tended garden may be nice enough, but if your partner spends most of his time hanging out with plants, you need to bring him down to earth. It may be okay for royalty to converse with green matter, but they don't have other things to do. By applying a little gentle persuasion, your partner will soon come round to the importance of re-assessing his priorities.

Full-Time Gardener

Dear: _____ *(name of husband or partner)*

Sometimes we watch you through the windows as you scurry round the garden tending to your beds/borders/fertilizers/growing bags/hybrids/pond liners/pole pruners/shredders/soil aerators/tool sets/and so on *(delete as applicable)*.

Come rain or shine, you're always out there lovingly nurturing hundreds of tiny miracle seeds, like a proud father looking after their every need. Which reminds me – the next time you spend a week in the garden, you might like to consider spending a few minutes of your valuable time with your family. Whilst you've been so busy outside, the rest of us are forced to compete with climbing beans/hose tidies/garden gnomes *(delete as applicable)* for attention.

We live in a state of relative poverty as a direct consequence of your ambitious landscaping projects, the last one costing a staggering £_____ *(state amount)*. In my view, this amounts to theft/embezzlement/dementia and warrants criminal investigation/summary justice/residential care *(delete as applicable)*.

You have _____ months/weeks/days/hours *(delete as applicable)* to overcome your gardening fixation. No doubt you'll find it difficult at first, spending time in the house with relative strangers. If you fail to comply with these terms, however, I can personally guarantee that you will wake up one morning in a state of shock on finding your hosepipe/sprinkler/antique water feature seriously vandalized.

Sincerely yours,

Sender:	Recipient:	Subject:	Category:
Female	Male	Lifestyle	Sending to Doghouse

Guidance Notes:

Ideal for:
Ending the madness

When the mere mention of 'home improvement' starts to cause panic, it's essential to make your reservations known. Once your home starts to lose value on an annual basis, it's time to act. You need to salvage what you can from the empty shell that used to be your home, and bar your partner from ever using his initiative again.

DIY

Dear: _____ *(name of husband or partner)*

Let me congratulate you on the effort you have put into various DIY projects over the past _____ *(state number)* years. I can honestly say that the home we moved into is now transformed/unrecognizable/structurally unsound *(delete as applicable)*.

There are a few minor things that I would like to draw to your attention.

Ever since you completed the re-wiring of the house, the light switch in the hall/landing/living room turns on the central heating/security alarm/immersion *(delete as applicable)*. And that's not all: I had no idea that by 'fixing' the shower/washing machine you could also inflict third-degree burns upon visiting relatives/magic the room into a swimming pool *(delete as applicable)*. For your next project, why not save yourself some time by stripping electrical wire with your teeth?

Your problem is that you don't actually have the skill to do anything yourself. You're probably still trying to find the:

☐ Code for the combination ladder
☐ Phone number for the wallpaper stripper
☐ Box for the jigsaw

Always playing around with your spray gun and your small parts, you need to master the basics of DIY such as changing a light bulb or installing a doormat before moving on to more advanced projects. If you're still determined to experiment with home improvement, why not try vacuuming/dusting/moving abroad *(delete as applicable)*.

Sincerely yours,

LETTER TO LOCAL AUTHORITY

Sender:	Recipient:	Subject:	Category:
Female	Male	Lifestyle	Sending to Doghouse

Guidance Notes:

Ideal for:
Dealing with nuisance

If members of your household are displaying antisocial behaviour, the least you can expect is for your local council to sort the problem out. Write them a letter, clearly detailing the problems and what you expect them to do about it. If you receive no response within a reasonable period (five years), take the matter to your local MP.

Letter to Local Authority

Dear Sir,

I am writing to inform you that my house has become a haven for demented and non-toilet-trained ANIMALS. You have powers to deal with nuisance and the duty to protect residents and animals alike.

The most anti-social of these beasts is *(please select one from the following)*:

☐ Neanderthal Man
☐ Homo Erectus
☐ Australopithecus Man

You can imagine my surprise when I recently discovered that I had been married to the above for twenty-odd years. The species can be recognized by the fact that they have a low IQ/are always playing with their tools/have difficulty communicating *(delete as applicable)*.

Additional ANIMALS include a Great Dane/Bull Terrier/mongrel/other _____ *(delete and state alternative if applicable)* that trashes the house and garden, and wears out the sofa by watching TV all day alongside the above.

They seem to be 'best friends' – always going on walks together and sharing many of the same interests. Like his canine accomplice, my husband shows real ability in scavenging for food/marking his territory/dribbling *(delete as applicable)*. Their social and domestic skills are equally diabolical.

I suggest that you take steps to REMOVE them both to a place of safety and experimentation ('safety' for the dog and 'experimentation' for the husband). No doubt the scientific community would give their collective right arm for the privilege of examining a live specimen dating back some 50,000 years/200,000 years/4 million years *(delete as applicable)*.

Please let me know when you are able to collect the above items.

Sincerely yours,

Little Angels

HOUSE RULES (SMALL CHILD)

Sender:	Recipient:	Subject:	Category:
Parent	Child	Lifestyle	Imposing Rules

Guidance Notes:

Ideal for: Establishing boundaries while you can

From the beginning, children should be given every encouragement to learn rules and boundaries, thus impressing upon them that an all-pervading sense of order prevails throughout the world. This will make it easier to attempt to bring your offspring's use of drugs and firearms under some sort of control when they become teenagers.

House Rules (Small Child)

1. The weekly price for the room is £_____, including Bed and Breakfast with liquidized meal, and may be refundable against future pocket-money credits.

2. The room will be tidied and sheets changed on _____ *(state day)* of each week.

3. Industrial-strength vocal chords should be used in moderation only, thereby permitting persons in other rooms to maintain their sanity whilst still being able to hear themselves speak.

4. Potty facilities shall be used during initial period of let until such time when communal bathroom facilities can be used in a responsible manner.

5. Parents or guardians reserve the right to move the child to another room without notice, or to an entirely separate part of the premises, including garage or loft.

6. The child shall not be permitted to destroy or consume any contents of the room including furniture, fixtures or fittings.

7. Musical instruments are prohibited and if found will be destroyed.

8. Friends with behavioural problems shall not be permitted on the premises.

9. Unaccompanied leave is strictly prohibited and is likely to result in the child being locked out of the house after the hour of 8 p.m.

10. Health and safety issues remain the responsibility of the child.

I, the undersigned, agree to all the above rules.

Child's signature or mark should be made below:

(insert date)

Sender:	Recipient:	Subject:	Category:
Parent	Child	Money	Asserting Rights

Guidance Notes:

Ideal for:
Lowering expectations

The pressure on parents to give ever more expensive gifts at Christmas is unyielding. Unless you take back control of the situation, you may suddenly find yourself emotionally blackmailed into giving away a yacht or holiday home to your ten-year-old. The best way to avoid this is to use the attached form, which places limits upon what your child can reasonably extort from you.

Christmas Present List

From: Santa Claus,
Greenland

To: _____ *(state name of child)*

I hope that this Christmas is going to be your best ever.

Having said that, there are lots of reasons why there will be a reduced Gift Service this season:

☐ An increase in world population

☐ The demand for more expensive gifts

☐ Melting snow

Consequently, it is no longer possible for an unlimited amount of presents to be handed out willy-nilly to all and sundry.

All orders must now be made through the completion of this form, which must be returned to the address above by _____ (dd/mm/yy).

Instructions:
Please enter your wish list clearly within the box below:

```
┌──────────────────────┐
│                      │
│                      │
│                      │
└──────────────────────┘
```

Terms & Conditions
You should note that the following will render your application void:

a) Writing outside the box
b) Incomplete sentences
c) Spelling mistakes
d) Scrawly writing

Signed by/For and on behalf of Santa Claus *(delete as applicable)*

Sender:	Recipient:	Subject:	Category:
Parent	Child	Money	Asserting Rights

Guidance Notes:

Ideal for:
Teaching financial prudence

Official sources suggest that the average cost of bringing up a child in today's world is an arm and a leg. Children should learn to apply for credit and be accountable for what they spend from an early age. This may seem obvious, but many parents dish out funds to ungrateful minors without scrutinizing how the money is spent. This pocket-money application form gets your child used to the world of credit, cash-flow, interest and form-filling almost from day one.

Pocket Money Claim Form

APPLICATION FOR CREDIT

To: *(insert name of parent or guardian)*

FOR THE APPLICANT TO COMPLETE:
(NO YELLOW CRAYON PLEASE)

Applicant's Name:*

Age in Whole Years: Sum of Pocket Money Required:

Term *(repayment period)*:   Interest Rate *(parent to fill in)*:

Reason for Application:

Please include a description, or drawing, of prospective item of purchase, where applicable.

Declaration:
'I confirm that an adult has explained to me the meaning of the term "legally binding document"'

Applicant's signature *(or mark)*:

FOR OFFICE USE ONLY:

Authorized/Not Authorized:

Reason for Rejection (unless arbitrary):

Date:

* 'Applicant's Name': an inability to supply this basic data in a legible form will render this application void.

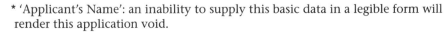

Sender:	Recipient:	Subject:	Category:
Parent	Child	Lifestyle	Imposing Rules

Guidance Notes:

Ideal for: Trying to re-establish boundaries

Adolescence is a difficult time, but the habitual misuse of drugs and firearms and other illegal or antisocial behaviour can be especially upsetting for a parent. An Acceptable Behaviour Contract or 'ABC' can help the responsible parent to reimpose boundaries before things get out of control.

Acceptable Behaviour Contract

PARTY (1): .... *(The 'Child')*

PARTY (2): .... *(The 'Parent')*

That PARTY (1) AGREES the following in respect of future conduct:

A. I will not draw graffiti or damage property inside the home.
B. I will not congregate in communal areas with the intention of threatening or intimidating innocent parties.
C. I will not listen to music of a nature or volume likely to, or calculated to, offend others.
D. I will not become intoxicated and upset other people with rude or offensive gestures.
E. I will not bring persons known or unknown to the home for the purpose of adolescent activities including full sex and other disturbances contrary to age of consent regulations.
F. I will not carry offensive weapons including loaded guns for the purpose of intimidating, bullying or extorting money or property from members of, or visitors to, the household.
G. I will not carry illicit drugs for the purpose of personal use or supply.

BREACH
THAT IF PARTY (1) does anything that he/she agrees not to do under this AGREEMENT, PARTY (2) will have no option but to apply for an ANTI-SOCIAL BEHAVIOUR ORDER or fill in a NOTICE OF ADOPTION.

Please sign and date below:

.... *(PARTY (1))*

.... *(PARTY (2))*

Sender:	Recipient:	Subject:	Category:
Parent	Child	Lifestyle	Launching Nuclear Strike

Guidance Notes:

Ideal for:
Doing your civic duty

With rights come responsibilities, and you have a responsibility to press charges if your child thinks they're above the law. Save public money by drafting the indictments yourself, and include as much forensic evidence as you can muster. An impending hearing can be a stressful time, so make sure you provide sympathy and understanding to your child prior to acting as chief witness for the prosecution.

Prosecuting Your Kids

INDICTMENTS AGAINST A JUVENILE

IN THE _____ COUNTY COURT   CLAIM NO: _____   DATE: _____

NAME OF THE ACCUSED: _____   *(son/daughter)*

THAT THE ABOVE IS CHARGED WITH THE FOLLOWING CRIMES:

COUNT 1

That on _____ (dd/mm/yy) the said child did cause CRIMINAL DAMAGE contrary to the Criminal Damage Act (1991) by:

☐ Spray-painting a motor vehicle belonging to the father of the accused with the legend
.... *(insert word or phrase)*.

☐ Putting the mother-in-law's glasses in the dishwasher.

☐ Conducting crash tests with the entire 'Vintage Classics' model-car collection belonging to the father of the accused by leaving them on the ....
.... *(state road or highway, e.g. A12)*.

COUNT 2

That on _____ (dd/mm/yy), contrary to the Road Traffic Act (1988), the said child did cause a breach of the peace by being found DRUNK IN CHARGE of a:

☐ Bicycle   ☐ Skateboard   ☐ Shopping trolley

COUNT 3

That on _____ (dd/mm/yy) the said child did carry a loaded weapon contrary to The Firearms Act (1968) with the purpose of:

☐ Extorting money from a local campaigning group called 'Pensioners Against Unjust Taxes'.

☐ Pursuing an 'entitlement' to a 'Baby-Bond Trust Fund' from the parents of the accused, whilst claiming that the fact that the scheme started some ten years after the said child's date of birth was irrelevant.

☐ Persuading the local newsagent to part with 'Lucky Dips' until the said child found a winning ticket.

COUNT 4

That the above child is responsible for a ruthless campaign of bullying contrary to the Anti-Social Behaviour Act (1990), although the parents of the accused have only now been willing to speak up.

THE SAID CHILD IS REQUIRED TO ATTEND THE CRIMINAL YOUTH COURT AT _____ *(State location)* ON _____ (DD/MM/YY) WHEN THE CASE AGAINST THE ACCUSED WILL BE HEARD.

COUNT 5

That between _____ and _____ *(insert dates)*, the said child never attended school and refused to co-operate with the Local Education Authority thereby causing the parents of the accused to:

☐ Be fined £ _____ *(insert amount)*.

☐ Be imprisoned for _____ days/weeks/months.

☐ Separate and pursue costly proceedings *against* custody.

Sender:	Recipient:	Subject:	Category:
Parent	Child	Lifestyle	Asserting Rights

Guidance Notes:

Ideal for:
Taking back control over your life

Not a step to be taken lightly, putting up a child for adoption or auction is a risky enterprise and should be used only as a last resort. Bear in mind that it is quite possible you will not be successful in your objective, and that an oversensitive child could well develop further insecurities should your intentions become known.

Notice of Adoption

NOTICE IS hereby given that the CHILD known as ....
.... *(insert name)* and whose date of birth is __/__/__
(dd/mm/yy) will be made available for ADOPTION on __/__/__ *(insert date)*.

Any person willing to ADOPT the said CHILD should please attend at the
following address to COLLECT the item:

....

....

(insert address)

WARNING is hereby given that any interested party should have:
• Infinite Patience
• Large and unwanted Large Sums Of Money
• Psychoanalysis

In the unlikely event that a number of persons of SOUND MIND come forward,
those persons shall be expected to BID in a SPECIAL AUCTION designed for the
purpose. NO minimum reserve price will be deemed to exist. BIDS must be made
in GOOD FAITH and items must be paid for and collected on the day –
irrespective of ERROR, MISTAKE, the misuse of drugs, etc. ALL ITEMS ARE SOLD
AS SEEN.

NO GUARANTEE or warranty will be deemed to exist and there is NO RIGHT OF
RETURN irrespective of condition or behaviour. NO LIABILITY will be accepted
for subsequent DESTRUCTION OF PROPERTY, INSANITY, BANKRUPTCY, LOSS
OF EARNINGS, BREAKDOWN OF RELATIONSHIP, etc.

At all times, FULL RESPONSIBILITY for the CHILD will reside solely with the NEW
OWNER/PARENT. At no time in the future will the CHILD be deemed to possess
any right to meet, contact or otherwise HARASS the child's former owner/parent
under any circumstances.

The current parents/owners should sign and date below:

....

CUSTODY AND ACCESS AGREEMENT

Sender:	Recipient:	Subject:	Category:
Parent	Child	Lifestyle	Asserting Rights

Guidance Notes:

Ideal for: Leaving on favourable terms

If the time has come when you and your partner need to live apart, your aim will be to settle delicate questions surrounding custody and access without handing over five years' salary to family lawyers. It's not difficult to engineer an agreement that puts your interests first and ensures access on your terms without the disruption and inconvenience associated with custody.

Custody and Access Agreement

This AGREEMENT is made BETWEEN:

(1) .... *(state male parent name)* and

(2) .... *(state female parent name)*

BOTH PARTIES wishing to lead separate lives, the following TERMS are hereby AGREED with respect to THE CHILD named .... *(state name)*:

1. That as a gesture of GENEROSITY, PARTY (1) renounces all claims of CUSTODY over the above and makes the same as a GIFT to PARTY (2) on condition that PARTY (1) shall enjoy UNFETTERED RIGHT of ACCESS but only when it shall suit his lifestyle and BUSY SCHEDULE.

2. Namely, it is HEREBY AGREED that PARTY (2) shall therefore be responsible for day-to-day tasks and associated running costs including, but NOT limited to, NAPPY-changing, POTTY-training, SICK disposal, PARASITE treatment, etc., and that in due course, PARTY (2) shall be solely responsible for strategies to combat temper TANTRUMS, antisocial behaviour, ASSAULT, ARSON, etc.

3. PARTY (1) shall enjoy ACCESS when desired, but probably not before the time when the said CHILD can COMMUNICATE in ways other than by screaming or effecting bodily discharge. Once this milestone has been reached, PARTY (1) shall from time to time COLLECT said CHILD for BIRTHDAY PARTIES, HOLIDAYS, FOOTBALL MATCHES, TRIPS to the ZOO, etc. It is FURTHER AGREED that if, at any time, the said CHILD becomes disagreeable or if PARTY (1) needs his own SPACE, PARTY (2) will COLLECT the said CHILD from any GPS coordinate within the hour.

Both PARTIES believing this to be a FAIR and EQUITABLE agreement confirm the same BELOW:

Signed and Dated: .... *(PARTY (1))*

Signed and Dated: .... *(PARTY (2))*

Sender:	Recipient:	Subject:	Category:
Child	Parent	Money	Asserting Rights

Guidance Notes:

Ideal for:
Asserting your rights

If you find that other kids at school get a better deal from their parents, enjoying quality holidays, entertainment systems and unlimited Internet access, you need to learn to be assertive. You should receive a childhood of at least an equal material standard to that of your peers, and you are entitled to use all available methods at your disposal to achieve your objective.

Parental Duties

To: _____ *(full name[s] of parent[s])*

Having conducted extensive research, I have come to the conclusion that your future parental duties should include the following goods and services, to be implemented within a realistic timescale (24 hours):

24-hours-a-day 'Direct, Any Destination', taxi service *('DAD' for short)*

Full consultation on holiday itineraries – with right of veto. Any air miles accumulated should be made available for my personal use.

Canteen-style home-food service with a choice of five 'balanced' options, including dishes high in saturated fat as well as a healthy salad alternative *(which I will never choose).*

Unlimited home shopping facility via Broadband. *(Please ensure that card supplied has a decent credit limit.)*

Unlimited sleepovers on offer with a programme of entertainment, including karaoke, etc. – staff should be motivated and properly qualified.

Subsidized bedroom-based home-entertainment system including a choice of games consoles and satellite TV.

Please note that entry to my bedroom is permitted only with express permission, except for the purpose of carrying out housework duties between the hours of __:__ and __:__ *(state times).*

Failure to comply with the above terms will GUARANTEE a call to CHILDLINE. No doubt you will have noticed the direct line recently installed in the hallway.

FREE USEFUL TIPS:

1. DON'T try to be funny in front of my friends
2. Trade in the retro wardrobe and get a STYLE consultant
3. Recycle the motor for scrap metal and get a PROPER CAR

PET OWNERSHIP SCHEME

Sender:	Recipient:	Subject:	Category:
Child	Parent	Lifestyle	Asserting Rights

Guidance Notes:

Ideal for: Getting what you want

Research has shown that pets can be important for a child's emotional development and well-being. If your parents know that you want a pet but stubbornly refuse to do anything about it, it may be time to take matters into your own hands. As soon as you get your pet home, explain that its welfare is paramount and that the whole family should share pet duties. With luck, you will have a friend for life – assuming you don't find something better on eBay.

Pet Ownership Scheme

To: .... *(name of parent or guardian)*

I have a RIGHT to own a pet of my choice, and as my parent you have a legal responsibility to look after it. My choice of pet is a:

☐ Goldfish   ☐ Hamster
☐ Canary   ☐ Rabbit
☐ Kitten   ☐ Puppy
☐ Iguana   ☐ Alligator

You will find the above species deposited in the living room/other

.... *(state location)*

in a box/plastic bag/small cage *(delete as applicable)*.

You have been allocated the following duties:

☐ Feeding my pet with a nutritionally balanced diet
☐ Paying for vets bills, counselling, behavioural therapy, etc.
☐ Dealing with any 'accidents' in an efficient but sensitive manner
☐ Taking my pet for walks as part of a proper exercise programme

I should warn you that failure to discharge any of the tasks above will be construed as wilful neglect amounting to cruelty, and I will have no option but to contact the appropriate authorities with instructions to prosecute.

It is important that my pet gets the very best start in life. On a purely voluntary basis, therefore, I will undertake to do all of the following:

•   Choose a name
•   Take its photograph
•   Dress it in silly clothes

All the best,

Signed and Dated:

....

NOTICE OF MUSIC FESTIVAL

Sender:	Recipient:	Subject:	Category:
Child	Parent	£ Money	Asserting Rights

Guidance Notes:

Ideal for:
Printing money

You have a right to stage major music events at home for financial gain. The key to commercial profitability in this sector is ruthless organization, right down to the last Portaloo. Don't bother with consultation: your parents will find it simpler if they're presented with a fait accompli detailing exactly what they have to do prior to leaving the area. After a couple of years, you should be able to set up a Limited Company and invite the major networks to tender for broadcasting rights.

Notice of Music Festival

NOTICE IS HEREBY given of a major music festival beginning on _____ (dd/mm/yy).

I am pleased to be able to confirm that the EVENT will take place within the grounds of *(insert full home address)*:

....

Any usual occupants of the PROPERTY except for 'the Organizers' will be required to RELOCATE. A 100-mile 'Exclusion Zone' will operate for the duration of the event, the duration being seven days.

It is with your interests in mind that I strongly recommend that the HOUSE should be cleared of all CLUTTER including photographs, memorabilia and ornaments. No responsibility will be accepted for consequent damage arising howsoever caused.

'The Organizers' would appreciate your help in ensuring that the GARAGE is properly provisioned for the occasion – to include a variety of ALCOHOL stacked to the ceiling, as well as DRUGS categorized and labelled 'A' to 'C' for quality-control purposes. I feel sure that you are as concerned as I am about the potential HEALTH AND SAFETY implications of young people being forced to trade illicit drugs of questionable quality – on our premises.

The GARDEN should be landscaped for the occasion and a STAGE erected to include a 1000W state-of-the-art SOUND SYSTEM with lighting equipment.

I am happy to work out the PRICING POLICY and security angle – whilst I suggest that you coordinate the construction of MOTORWAY SIGNS to the event, handle RADIO PROMOTION and arrange for the installation of PORTALOOS.

Thank you for the interest you have shown by reading this NOTICE. You will be impressed to learn that 'the Organizers' anticipate an ANNUAL event – especially given the enthusiasm shown by niche bands such as DEATH'S HEAD and ANARCHY NOW.

Signed and dated: *('The Organizers')*

....

Sender:	Recipient:	Subject:	Category:
Child	Parent	Money	Launching Nuclear Strike

Guidance Notes:

Ideal for: Compensation for neglect

It is your parents' responsibility to bring you up to be a success in every way. If you emerge from adolescence an awkward, inadequate, confused and antisocial teenager, you know where to point the finger of blame. The only people who have made it their life's work to bring you into the world confident and secure are your parents. When it becomes obvious that they have failed, it's payback time, and the tedious 'nature verses nurture' debate is completely irrelevant: whether the failure comes down to genes or upbringing, your parents are still to blame.

Cheque №
863747
863747

Suing your Parents

PLEASE DO NOT USE CRAYON WHEN FILLING IN THIS FORM
CLAIM FOR COMPENSATION

IN THE .... COUNTY COURT

CLAIM NO: .... DATE: ....

Type of Claim: OPEN-SHUT CASE

1. NAME OF CLAIMANT .... *(insert your name here)*

2. NAME OF DEFENDANT (1) .... *(insert name of parent)*

   NAME OF DEFENDANT (2) .... *(insert name of parent)*

3. PARTICULARS OF CLAIM:

3.1 THAT THE DEFENDANTS GAVE LIFE TO THE CLAIMANT DESPITE INSUFFICIENT FINANCIAL MEANS OR PROSPECTS, ENSURING:

☐ SOCIO-ECONOMIC DISADVANTAGE
☐ THE HABITUAL INGESTION OF ADDITIVE-LADEN JUNK FOOD
☐ BEING FORCED TO ATTEND A RUBBISH SCHOOL
☐ CRAP TRAINERS

3.2 THAT THE DEFENDANTS KNOWINGLY PASSED ON 'LOSER' GENES INCLUDING:

☐ UGLY PHYSICAL CHARACTERISTICS
☐ LOW IQ
☐ LACK OF CHARM

3.3 THAT THE DEFENDANTS LACKED BASIC PARENTING SKILLS, AND IN PARTICULAR, THAT THEY FAILED TO:

☐ GIVE SUFFICIENT ATTENTION TO THE CLAIMANT – LEADING TO 'ADD' (ATTENTION DEFICIT DISORDER)
☐ DISCOVER PRODIGIOUS TALENT IN THE CLAIMANT AT AN EARLY AGE WHICH WOULD HAVE ENSURED CHILD STARDOM AND A TV CAREER
☐ FAILED TO GIVE CONSTANT AND UNCONDITIONAL PRAISE LEADING TO 'ASED' (ACUTE SELF-ESTEEM DEFICIT)

Suing your Parents (Continued)

NAME OF CLAIMANT	*(insert your name here)*
NAME OF DEFENDANT (1)	*(insert name of parent)*
NAME OF DEFENDANT (2)	*(insert name of parent)*

4. PRINCIPAL GROUNDS

THE FACTORS DETAILED ABOVE AMOUNT TO NEGLECT CONTRARY TO:

☐ COMMON LAW
☐ STATUTE
☐ UNIVERSAL HUMAN RIGHTS

AND THAT THIS FAILURE ADVERSELY AFFECTED THE CLAIMANT'S INDIVIDUAL AND SOCIAL DEVELOPMENTAL NORMS THEREBY CAUSING:

☐ BULLYING (OF SELF OR OTHER PEOPLE)
☐ EXPULSION FROM SCHOOL
☐ SOCIAL EXCLUSION

AND THAT THIS CHAIN OF EVENTS CAUSED CHRONIC UNDERACHIEVEMENT AND DISAFFECTION LEADING TO:
COMPLEX PERSONALITY DISORDERS IN THE CASE OF THE CLAIMANT AND FAILURE TO GET A GIRLFRIEND/BOYFRIEND.

5. QUANTUM

5.1 EMBARRASSMENT, PAIN AND SUFFERING   £ _____ *(Insert amount)*

5.2 LOSS OF EARNINGS   £ _____ *(Insert amount)*

5.3 PUNITIVE DAMAGES   £ _____ *(Insert amount)*

5.4 TOTAL   £ _____ *(Insert amount)*

I DECLARE THAT THE INFORMATION ON THIS FORM IS TRUE

Signed and Dated:
....

THE DEFENDANT SHOULD EITHER PAY THE AMOUNT CLAIMED IN (5.4) WITHIN 14 DAYS, OR SERVE NOTICE THAT THE CLAIM IS TO BE DEFENDED WHICH COULD CARRY ADDITIONAL COURT COSTS

Endgame

Sender:	Recipient:	Subject:	Category:
Male	Female	Work	Asserting Rights

Guidance Notes:

Ideal for:
Ending a relationship

By this point, you should have:

- Set out the standards required in the signed and witnessed 'Cohabitation Agreement' (see page 23)
- Documented breaches and worked tirelessly towards getting your partner 'back on track'
- Explored the possibility of further training without success

You are now in a position to give Notice of Dismissal to your wife or girlfriend. Note that the 'right of appeal' is nothing more than a formality.

Notice of Dismissal (Performance)

Dear: .... *(name of wife or partner)*

As various assessments have shown, you have failed to carry out your duties to the standards required. It is hardly necessary to report that over time there has been little or no improvement.

Considerable effort and resources have been spent on training in the hope that this would enable you to meet your targets, but to no avail. Attempts to find new areas of expertise in which you might excel have proved futile.

This leaves me with no alternative but to terminate our relationship with immediate effect as of .... (dd/mm/yy). You are required to remove your person and your belongings from your former home. May I suggest that you do this under cover of darkness so as not to cause a scene.

It is my duty to remind you that you have the right to appeal against this decision, even though it has been reached fairly and in accordance with procedures that you should have known about. If you wish to appeal, you need to produce new evidence, along with your fee of £212.25.

I should like to take this opportunity to thank you for all your past efforts. Your record aside, you have contributed fully to the team and I wish you every success for the future.

Sincerely yours,

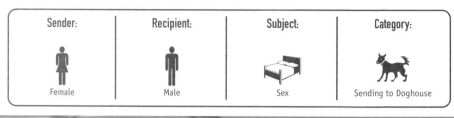

Sender:	Recipient:	Subject:	Category:
Female	Male	Sex	Sending to Doghouse

Guidance Notes:

Ideal for:
Ending a relationship

If your boyfriend or husband can't last the distance, you may need to draw on your reserves of tact and sensitivity to address this common problem. You might have made the reasonable assumption in the early days that things would improve once the initial excitement experienced by your partner in having a new girlfriend began to wear off. But if the problem has persisted, you will have to insist on your partner taking responsibility and seeking help. Remember that you have a right to a half-decent sex life, and this letter explains why termination may be the only realistic option.

Notice of Dismissal
(Time Management)

Dear: *(name of husband or partner)*

At our meeting on _____ (dd/mm/yy), we discussed your continuing failure in the area of time management. It was agreed that your performance has fallen far short of a reasonable standard, and that this has had a severely damaging effect on our relationship.

The problem of 'arriving early' has become habitual. I have calculated that your average time during intercourse before ejaculation is:_____ *(insert number)* minutes/seconds *(delete as applicable)*.

And, further, that in _____ % *(insert value)* of cases, release is immediately followed by a state of unconsciousness. This state of affairs provides me with no interest/enjoyment/ will to go on *(delete as applicable)*.

Your modest size, in fairness being due to genetic failings, would not in itself be sufficient grounds for termination. However, the combination of insignificant impact with an adolescent style of delivery is conclusive.

I note that no reasonable efforts have been made to correct the problem despite the possibilities of psychoanalysis and surgery. Your shortcomings leave me with no alternative but to terminate the relationship forthwith.

Sincerely yours,

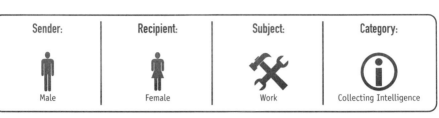

Sender:	Recipient:	Subject:	Category:
Male	Female	Work	Collecting Intelligence

Guidance Notes:

Ideal for:
Sharing information

When a business wishes to take on someone new, an employer will usually seek a reference in order to gain useful information about a candidate. Human sensibilities mean that this is not standard practice within the area of relationships, but you may still wish to forward a reference to her new place of work as a gesture of goodwill.

Reference for Ex-Partner

Dear: _____ *(ex-partner's new partner/boyfriend)*

Re: _____ *(name of ex-partner)*

I have recently been provided with your name and contact details by the above. It is my understanding that your premises will be her new place of work.

Although you had not requested a reference as such, it is my guess that relevant information will be useful for you in ensuring that her first day, being _____ (dd/mm/yy), goes as smoothly as possible. By this, I do not wish to imply that your best option is damage limitation. I am sure you would agree, however, that openness and transparency is to everyone's advantage in this matter – and it is with this in mind that I submit the following:

I can confirm that _____ *(name of ex-partner)* has worked with me for a period of _____ weeks/months/years/decades *(delete as applicable)*. The overall standard of work has been inconsistent/disappointing/ negligent and her general attitude has been disinterested/hostile/ malevolent *(delete as applicable)*.

As with any candidate, there have been particular areas of weakness, which I would summarize as follows:

_____

_____

_____

(continue on additional sheets as necessary)

It is my devout hope that the above proves to be a surprising success in all areas of her work.

Yours sincerely,

_____

Sender:	Recipient:	Subject:	Category:
Female	Male	Health	Sending to Doghouse

Guidance Notes:

Ideal for: Institutionalizing your loved one

It's a sad fact that many of us will spend our twilight years in a care home. Coming to terms with the end of independent living can often be painful, and sometimes it will take a partner or other relative to force the issue. Relevant factors may include a declining quality of life and its impact upon others. The scenario of a man in the prime of his life requiring institutionalization can be particularly difficult to face up to, but it may also be the only way forward for all concerned.

Care Home Letter of Referral

Dear: *(Proprietor of care home)*
....

Re: *(Name and DOB of husband or partner)*
....

It is with some regret that I write to you, but I feel that the time has come when my partner would benefit from the services you are able to provide.

On paper at least, you will notice that the above subject is still a relatively young man – being in his 20s/30s/40s *(delete as applicable)*. There is nothing wrong with him physically, although I can confirm that he has a condition known as pig-ignorance.

Unfortunately, I am no longer able to cope for the following reasons:

- ☐ He doesn't wash or attend to bodily hygiene
- ☐ He communicates in grunts
- ☐ He is rude to everyone he meets
- ☐ He watches telly all day
- ☐ He is apparently incapable of work
- ☐ He is noisy and smelly
- ☐ He can't remember anything

It is a real weight off my mind knowing that you will be able to care for
.... *(name of partner)* on a permanent basis. I will be depositing him on your premises with his personal effects on .... (dd/mm/yy).

Yours sincerely,

....

Sender:	Recipient:	Subject:	Category:
Male	Female	£ Money	Launching Nuclear Strike

Guidance Notes:

Ideal for:
Securing your future

It's not unusual for many years to go by before you finally realize the scale of the devastation attributable to a failed relationship. If you can prove, on the balance of probabilities, that it's all been your partner's fault – common sense says you should be entitled to compensation. This form claims settlement on three different grounds plus punitive damages in order to maximize the value of your claim. You won't turn the clock back, but you will be able to plan for the future with greater confidence and security.

Suing your Partner

CLAIM FOR COMPENSATION

IN THE .... COUNTY COURT   CLAIM NO: DATE: ....

---

1. NAME OF CLAIMANT .... *(insert your name)*

2. NAME OF DEFENDANT .... *(insert name of partner)*

---

3.   PARTICULARS OF CLAIM

3.1   THAT THE DEFENDANT ENTRAPPED THE CLAIMANT BY THE FOLLOWING MEANS:

3.2   SHE WORE MAKE-UP WHICH MADE HER LOOK YOUNGER AND MORE ATTRACTIVE THAN SHE REALLY WAS

3.3   BY BEING HELPFUL AND ATTENTIVE IN THE EARLY DAYS, SHE GAVE THE IMPRESSION THAT THIS WAS A PERMANENT AS OPPOSED TO A TEMPORARY STATE

3.4   THAT AS A DIRECT CONSEQUENCE OF THE ABOVE DEVICES, THE CLAIMANT ENTERED INTO A RELATIONSHIP THAT HE WOULD NOT HAVE OTHERWISE ENTERTAINED

3.5   THAT ONCE THE MISTAKE HAD BEEN REALIZED, A COMMITMENT HAD ALREADY BEEN MADE AND IT BECAME IMPOSSIBLE FOR THE CLAIMANT TO TAKE EFFECTIVE CORRECTIVE ACTION

3.6   THE DEFENDANT SUFFERED LOSSES AS A DIRECT RESULT OF THE ABOVE AND IS THEREFORE ENTITLED TO COMPENSATION FROM THE DEFENDANT

4.   PRINCIPAL GROUNDS

4.1   THAT COMPENSATION IS DUE FOR LOSS OF EARNINGS BETWEEN _____ AND _____ *(state years)* – COMPRISING AN AVERAGE ANNUAL FINANCIAL HAEMORRHAGE OF _____ *(state amount)*, WITH MONEY SPENT ON SHOES, CLOTHES, COSMETICS, ETC.

4.2   THAT COMPENSATION IS ALSO DUE FOR WASTED YEARS RELATING TO THE SAME PERIOD – BASED ON A NOMINAL SETTLEMENT OF _____ *(state amount)* PER ANNUM

4.3   THAT COMPENSATION IS FURTHER DUE FOR PSYCHOLOGICAL DAMAGE ALSO RELATING TO THE STATED PERIOD – BASED ON ADDITIONAL EXPENDITURE INCURRED BY THE CLAIMANT ON PSYCHIATRIC TREATMENT, MEDICATION, HYPNOTHERAPY AND ALCOHOL

5.   QUANTUM

5.1   LOSS OF EARNINGS   £ .... *(Insert amount)*

5.2   WASTED YEARS   £ .... *(Insert amount)*

5.3   PSYCHOLOGICAL DAMAGE   £ .... *(Insert amount)*

5.4   PUNITIVE DAMAGES   £ .... *(Insert amount)*

5.5   TOTAL   £ .... *(Insert amount)*

I DECLARE THAT THE INFORMATION ON THIS FORM IS TRUE

Signed and Dated:

....

THE DEFENDANT SHOULD EITHER PAY THE AMOUNT CLAIMED IN 5.5 WITHIN 14 DAYS OR SERVE NOTICE THAT THE CLAIM IS TO BE DEFENDED, WHICH COULD CARRY ADDITIONAL COURT COSTS

Sender:	Recipient:	Subject:	Category:
		£	
Female	Male	Money	Launching Nuclear Strike

Guidance Notes:

Ideal for: Putting the record straight

There are never enough hours in the day at the best of times, and the last thing you should have to put up with is dealing with a Claim for Compensation issued by your partner in the County Court. You may be seriously tempted just to ignore it and hope for the best, but it's better to issue your own Counter Claim and demand a five-day hearing. This way, you'll get the opportunity to give a long-winded account of everything you've had to put up with and no one will be able to interrupt. Should the case go against you, make sure you appeal to the European Court in order to exploit the publicity and go shopping in Belgium.

Counter Claim

COUNTER CLAIM FOR COMPENSATION
Type of Claim: **FULL-SCALE RETALIATION**

IN THE   COUNTY COURT   CLAIM NO: DATE:

---

1. NAME OF CLAIMANT   *(insert your name)*

2. NAME OF DEFENDANT   *(insert name of partner)*

---

3.   **PARTICULARS OF CLAIM** *(otherwise known as 'the full hairdryer treatment')*:
AT THE BEGINNING I THOUGHT YOU HAD AN UNUSUAL SENSE OF HUMOUR AND A CERTAIN ECCENTRICITY BUT NOW I REALIZE YOU'RE JUST NUTS. WHEN I THINK OF THE TIMES I'VE TRIED TO EXPLAIN TO YOU THE SIMPLEST THINGS I WONDER WHETHER YOU EVER LISTEN LIKE THE IMPORTANCE OF BUDGETING WHEN YOU'VE GOT RESPONSIBILITIES DO I HAVE TO REMIND YOU OF THE COUNTLESS TIMES YOU'VE SPENT OUR ENTIRE MONTHLY INCOME BEFORE ANY BILLS HAVE BEEN PAID WHEN I THINK OF THE TIME I'VE PUT INTO THIS FAMILY WITH NO HELP FROM YOU I WONDER WHERE MY LIFE'S GONE AND NOW THIS TO BE HONEST IF IT HADN'T BEEN FOR YOU I COULD HAVE HAD A REWARDING CAREER OF MY OWN GAINING FINANCIAL INDEPENDENCE SELF-RESPECT AND THE CONFIDENCE TO TELL LOSERS LIKE YOU EXACTLY WHERE TO GO.
(CONTINUE IN THE SAME VEIN BY INSERTING ADDITIONAL SHEETS AS NECESSARY)

4.   **PRINCIPAL GROUNDS**
4.1   BY ACTING AS FULL-TIME 'NANNY' TO THE BOY WHO NEVER GREW UP
4.2   BY ACTING AS FULL-TIME 'NURSE' TO THE MAN WHO GETS A LIFE-THREATENING CONDITION KNOWN AS A COLD AND HAS TO STAY IN BED ALL DAY ON A DAILY BASIS
4.3   BY ACTING AS FULL-TIME 'SPEECH THERAPIST' TO THE NEANDERTHAL MAN WHO HAS YET TO LEARN THE ART OF REAL-TIME CONVERSATION
4.4   BY ACTING AS FULL-TIME 'PAINTER AND DECORATOR' AND CONSULTANT CIVIL ENGINEER AFTER YOUR DIY ATTEMPTS GO WRONG

5.   **QUANTUM**
COMPENSATION IS DUE FOR LOSS OF EARNINGS BETWEEN _____ AND _____ *(state years)*
CALCULATED ON THE BASIS OF AN AVERAGE FULL-TIME SALARY FOR THE FOLLOWING:

5.1   NANNY @ £16,000 pa   £   *(Insert amount)*

5.2   NURSE @ 20,000 pa   £   *(Insert amount)*

5.3   SPEECH THERAPIST @ £30,000 pa   £   *(Insert amount)*

5.4   PAINTER AND DECORATOR @ £60,000 pa   £   *(Insert amount)*

5.5   CONSULTANCY FEES (CIVIL ENGINEER)   £   *(Insert amount)*

6   **TOTAL**   £   *(Insert amount)*

I DECLARE THAT THE INFORMATION ON THIS FORM IS TRUE
(DEFENDANT SHOULD SIGN BELOW)

Signed and Dated:

Sender:	Recipient:	Subject:	Category:
Male/Female	Mother-in-law	Health	Asserting Rights

Guidance Notes:

Ideal for: Preparing for the worst

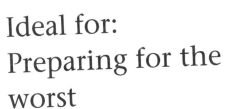

Sadly, many people forget to express their wishes to their family towards the close of play. Death is a subject difficult to broach, and yet a 'living will' can help your mother-in-law to achieve a dignified exit, and one which also spares those in the immediate vicinity unnecessary pain and suffering. Appointing a Health Care Proxy can bring things to a speedier conclusion. It will also save the public purse from spending valuable resources which would be better spent on people who have a brighter future to look forward to.

Living Will

Name: *(The Mother-In-Law)*

Address: *(The Dragon's Den)*

I CONFIRM that I am of sound mind and hereby make this ADVANCE DIRECTIVE on future medical care. I wish it to bind my family, my doctor, and anyone else unfortunate enough to be around when it becomes clear that I am a sandwich short of a picnic.

I HEREBY appoint my son-/daughter-in-law Health Care Proxy and give him/her authority to make decisions on my behalf when he/she judges that the lights are on but no one's home.

MEDICAL TREATMENT I DO NOT WANT:

I REFUSE medical treatment to unnecessarily prolong my life where, in the view of my son-/daughter-in-law:
This would not be cost-effective, or
It would be unfair on other people

MEDICAL TREATMENT I DO WANT:

I DO wish to receive powerful drugs that will suppress my power of speech so as to prevent me from talking endlessly about my ailments and complaints.

IT IS MY INTENTION that this document be irrevocable despite the inevitable torrent of delusional protests for which I apologize in advance to all concerned.

[Note to son-/daughter-in-law: fold document over on dotted line before requesting signature]

- -

Signature: Date:

Witness's Signature: Date:

EXCLUSION ORDER (MOTHER-IN-LAW)

Sender:	Recipient:	Subject:	Category:
Male/Female	Mother-in-law	Health	Launching Nuclear Strike

Guidance Notes:

Ideal for: Removing the problem

You'll be relieved to know that legislation against antisocial behaviour have been increased considerably in recent years. If you need a break from your mother-in-law in order to maintain some degree of sanity, you should remove the problem by applying for an injunction in the form of an Exclusion Order. The Courts are usually all too familiar with persistent offenders, and you may find that you have the full sympathy of the judge from the word go.

Exclusion Order
(Mother-In-Law)

APPLICATION FOR AN ORDER

IN THE .... COUNTY COURT   CLAIM NO: DATE: ....

EXCLUDING THE DEFENDANT FROM ENTERING A SPECIFIC AREA
OR REGION

NAME OF APPLICANT: .... *(son-/daughter-in-law)*

NAME OF DEFENDANT: .... *(mother-in-law)*

PARTICULARS OF CLAIM
THAT THE APPLICANT HUMBLY PETITIONS THE COURT FOR AN ORDER PROHIBITING
THE DEFENDANT MOTHER-IN-LAW FROM:
(A) ENTERING THE CLAIMANT'S MATRIMONIAL HOME
(B) ENTERING THE LOCALITY KNOWN AS: ....
(Insert details e.g. east of England)

PRINCIPAL GROUNDS
THAT THE DEFENDANT MOTHER-IN-LAW HAS DISPLAYED CATEGORY 'A' ANTI-SOCIAL
BEHAVIOUR OVER A PERIOD OF _____ YEARS CAUSING WIDESPREAD DAMAGE TO
QUALITY OF LIFE, EMOTIONAL TRAUMA, ETC., AS EVIDENCED BY DIARY SHEETS, TAPE
RECORDINGS, ETC., CONTAINED WITHIN THE COURT'S OWN CATALOGUE OF FILES:
VOL. NOS. _____ *(Complete as applicable)*.

(1) THAT SHE COMES ROUND UNINVITED, MOVES INTO THE BATHROOM AND TREATS
THE HOME AS HER OWN (2) THAT SHE REGULARLY GOES INTO A TIDYING-UP FRENZY,
'LOSING' THINGS BY THROWING THEM AWAY (3) THAT SHE ACTS AS A TV-STYLE HOME
MAKEOVER CONSULTANT BY PROCEEDING TO REARRANGE THE ENTIRE HOUSE
WITHOUT OBTAINING PRIOR CONSENT.

SPECIAL NOTICE OF UNITED NATIONS INVOLVEMENT
THE COURT'S ATTENTION IS DRAWN TO THE CLAIMANT'S RECENT APPEAL TO THE
UNITED NATION'S 'ARMED INTERVENTION COMMITTEE' FOLLOWING SUCCESSFUL
PLANNING PERMISSION BEING GRANTED TO THE DEFENDANT MOTHER-IN-LAW TO
BUILD A 'GRANNY FLAT' ADJACENT TO THE CLAIMANT'S PROPERTY. IT IS THE
CLAIMANT'S CONTENTION THAT OPERATION 'DRAGON'S DEN' MUST NOT BE
ALLOWED TO SUCCEED AS IT WILL HAVE A DESTABILIZING EFFECT ON THE REGION.

I, THE CLAIMANT, HEREBY DECLARE THAT THE INFORMATION ON THIS FORM IS TRUE

Signed and Dated: ....

Sender:	Recipient:	Subject:	Category:
Male/Female	Mother-in-law	Money	Launching Nuclear Strike

Guidance Notes:

Ideal for:
Retributive justice

If you feel that your mother-in-law has ruined your life, why not try to obtain a fair level of compensation in the county court? The approach might be untested, but a landmark case could win you lucrative publicity. Never underestimate your enemy, however: your mother-in-law is likely to have a crack legal team seeking to win the case on a technicality. Nevertheless, a case won can be uniquely satisfying and may result in humiliation, penury and homelessness for the defendant. Even if the odds are long, it may be worth a serious investment in time and energy.

Suing your Mother-In-Law

CLAIM FOR COMPENSATION

IN THE .... COUNTY COURT   CLAIM NO: DATE: ....

Type of Claim: **VINDICTIVE BUT JUST**

1. NAME OF CLAIMANT *(son-/daughter-in-law)*
....

2. NAME OF DEFENDANT *(mother-in-law)*
....

PARTICULARS OF CLAIM

THAT FOLLOWING THE UNFORTUNATE BREACH BETWEEN THE PARTIES OF THE FORMER MATRIMONIAL HOME, IT IS THE CLAIMANT'S BELIEF THAT THE DEFENDANT IS RESPONSIBLE FOR THE RESULTANT PSYCHOLOGICAL TRAUMA, FINANCIAL RUIN AND FAMILY DISLOCATION.

PRINCIPAL GROUNDS

THAT THE ABOVE STATE OF AFFAIRS HAS BEEN CAUSED BY THE DEFENDANT MOTHER-IN-LAW BY THE FOLLOWING MEANS:

- TALKING ABOUT NOTHING AT A SPEED OF 20 WORDS PER SECOND AND IN PERSON, OVER THE TELEPHONE, CAUSING DISTRESS AND POST-TRAUMATIC STRESS DISORDER.
- COERCING THE PANICKED CLAIMANT INTO BUYING NEW KITCHENS, BATHROOMS AND CONSERVATORIES AT ABSURD PRICES TO CREATE A SHOW-HOME WHICH IS NOW A NO-HOME.
- THAT THE ABOVE FACTORS HAVE COMBINED TO CAUSE MULTIPLE BREAKDOWNS AND DOMESTIC ARMAGEDDON.

QUANTUM

POST-TRAUMATIC STRESS DISORDER	£	*(Insert amount)*
FINANCIAL RUIN	£	*(Insert amount)*
FAMILY DISLOCATION	£	*(Insert amount)*
TOTAL	£	*(Insert amount)*

I, THE CLAIMANT, DECLARE THAT THE INFORMATION ON THIS FORM IS TRUE

Signed and Dated: ....

THE DEFENDANT SHOULD EITHER PAY THE AMOUNT CLAIMED WITHIN 14 DAYS OR SERVE NOTICE THAT THE CLAIM IS TO BE DEFENDED, WHICH COULD CARRY ADDITIONAL COURT COSTS

Sender:	Recipient:	Subject:	Category:
Mother-in-law	Male/Female	Health	Launching Nuclear Strike

Guidance Notes:

Ideal for:
Achieving closure

You may feel that your son-in-law or daughter-in-law has simply gone too far this time, and that only an extreme solution will suffice. Should you feel the urge to do violence, perhaps first consider therapy before getting your hands dirty. Alternatively, you could pay someone else to do the job for you. Whilst such an action isn't condoned, it's still important to draft a decent letter. Remember not to keep a copy for your records.

Letter to Arrange a 'Contract'

Dear: *(Proprietor of Agency)*

Re: *(Name of Son-/Daughter-in-Law)*

I was pleased to obtain your contact details which I acquired via a friend/recommendation/Internet/other *(delete as applicable)*. I confirm that I am a new/returning customer *(delete as applicable)*.

I am writing to you because I wish to take out a 'contract' on the above. I have read and understood your terms and conditions. I do/do not wish to take advantage of the Tragic Accident Guarantee Option. I am/am not entitled to the Pensioners' Discount of 15% off the advertised price *(delete as applicable)*.

As per your terms, I have today electronically transferred the sum of £............ *(state amount)* into Swiss Bank Account No. _ _ _ _ _ _ _ _ _ _ _ _ with Sort Code: _ _ - _ _ - _ _. The same amount will be deposited into the same account within 24 hours of the successful completion of the job.

I can now confirm that at .... hrs G.M.T. *(state time)* on .... (dd/mm/yy), the subject will be located at ....
....*

I enclose a photograph of the above for your convenience which should/should not be returned to me on completion of the job for sentimental/other reasons *(delete as applicable)*.

You have not received this letter.

Yours sincerely,

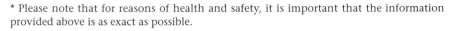

* Please note that for reasons of health and safety, it is important that the information provided above is as exact as possible.